Collective Ownership Based Economy

Collective Ownership Based Economy

A ROAD MAP TO PROSPERITY, PEACE, AND HAPPINESS FOR ALL

Prathapchandra Kedilaya

Acknowledgments to
Priya Dodwad
and
Sumanth Kedilaya
(in alphabetical order),
for editing the manuscript;
Kalpana Hebbar,
for art picture on the back cover;
and
Veena Sukumar
for drawing cartoon art

Preface

CAPITALISM OR MARKET ECONOMY IS the socioeconomic system currently in practice all over the world, including in the so-called socialist and communist countries, and it has been so for a long time. The roots of the capitalist economy evolved naturally since prehistoric times out of historical accidents. It is not that one day a group of wise folks from different parts of the world sat together, thought through, conceived, and adopted this system.

The fundamental and central feature of the capitalist economy is *private ownership of the wealth* of society. All other features of capitalism are the consequence of this central feature. Capitalism, therefore, may rightly be called *private ownership based economy* (POBE).

Social scientists have now recognized that the capitalist economy is defective—unscientific and inefficient. The main adverse social consequence of this defect is *material scarcity* for the majority despite having enough natural resources in society. Other unfavorable effects are unscrupulous scramble for the accumulation of wealth and the resulting inter-human competition, conflicts, and violence. The capitalist economy is considered the root cause of all the existing human ills and sufferings at both social and individual levels—not just for the poor, but also for the rich.

Since a couple of centuries ago, social scientists have been proposing a *socialist model* of the economy, with its many versions, as a better alternative to capitalism. The common central tenet of all these versions is *collective ownership* or *common ownership of society's wealth by all its members.* Socialist economy, therefore, may be called *collective ownership based economy* (**COBE**) similar to how capitalism may be called private ownership based economy (**POBE**).

Notable socialist movements that are actively involved at present are *Communism, World Socialist Movement, The Venus Project,* and *The Zeitgeist Movement.* The central tenet of all these economic models is *collective ownership* of wealth.

At present, socialist economies are misunderstood and misrepresented, and are associated with low popularity and stigma. It is mainly because the "communist" nations, past and present, have not adopted the twin principal tenets of a truly socialist economy—*collective ownership of wealth* and *democracy.*

The economic model proposed in this book resembles the existing models of socialist economic systems a lot. The model is called "*Collective Ownership Based Economy*" (**COBE**) because '*collective ownership*' is the central tenet of a truly socialist economic model.

However, the proposed **COBE** model, unlike other socialist models, strongly endorses democracy; it believes that the new economic order can be established in a single country in isolation;

it is of the view that the establishment of the new economy needs not to wait until the collapse of capitalism.

An *ideal society* is the one where all its members enjoy prosperity, peace, and happiness.

The ideas presented in the book aim at establishing an ideal society by bringing about a fundamental structural change in the socioeconomic system. These ideas are in no way utopian, nor do they require rocket science to realize them. They are realistic, practicable goals requiring only the intelligent application of what we already know.

Adopting the policy of collective ownership of wealth means providing enormous benefit in terms of attaining material abundance and enhancement of leisure for people. This benefit is because of economies of scale, which is the most fundamental economic principle, though not pointed out hitherto by any of the advocates of socialist or socialist like economic models.

Find in this book the answers for the following questions and more: How an economic system conditions human behavior? How have humans evolved to end up with the current capitalist economic system? How, by replacing the current system with the proposed COBE, would the society achieve—material abundance, enhancement of human leisure, economic and sexual emancipation, elimination of human greed, hatred, ego, envy, superstitions, political corruption, crime, war, the establishment of world society, and so on? Also find in the book suggestions for further reforms in *democracy*, and an *action plan to establish COBE.*

"It is now highly feasible to take care of everybody on earth at a 'higher standard of living than any have ever known'. It no longer has to be you or me. Selfishness is unnecessary and henceforth unrationalizable as mandated by survival. War is obsolete."—R. Buckminster Fuller

The societal system determines the fate of every member of society. It is not the other way, like some say "The society changes, only if every member of it changes".

"If solutions within the system are so impossible to find, maybe we should change the system itself." —Greta Thunberg, Climate activist

Keywords: collective ownership based economy, democracy, democratic socialism, economic ideology, economic system, political ideology, politico-economic system, socialism

Contents

Human Beings Are Unique and Superanimals in Many Ways with Respect to Other Species

HUMANS ARE BIOLOGICALLY OR GENETICALLY highly evolved animals in terms of learning, rationality, intelligence, abstract thinking, problem-solving, toolmaking, creativity, sociability, and communication skill. They have invented the written language that enables them to spread information and knowledge at a given time and over generations. They have developed science and technology to unimaginable levels. They have even invented democracy. In these matters, humans are in a unique place compared to other species, which are nowhere near them.

Does it automatically mean that all is well with human life at present? It doesn't look so and hasn't been looking so for a long time. Human's outstanding advancement in scientific technology has not been accompanied by an equal scientific development in social sciences, particularly in the socio-economic-political field.

An adage goes like this: "Man can now fly in the air like a bird and swim under the ocean like a fish. Now, if only he could walk the earth like a man on the land, this would be paradise".

Humans have the potential, all right, but it appears like they have not utilized their potential to the full and somehow lost their way somewhere, long ago.

CHAPTER 2

Prevailing Human Ailments

THE MAJORITY OF HUMANS AT present suffer from destitution, homelessness, hunger, poverty, unemployment, debt, superstitions, and preventable diseases—communicable and lifestyle diseases. Even the rich are haunted by economic insecurity.

Besides, almost all people are affected by interpersonal discords, family discords, and mental stress.

At the societal level, humans are facing problems like natural calamities, political corruption, crimes, drugs, terrorism, and international wars.

All these ills have been with human beings for a long time.

Recent additions to the societal ills are overpopulation, depletion of natural resources, scarcity of clean water and renewable energy, environmental pollution, global warming, and ecological imbalance.

These are all ongoing human problems, and the picture looks grim. It is not just that you don't want to be a sufferer in this sick society. It is also that you are bound to feel sick when you see others suffering even if you are living luxurious and comfortable life.

Are these human ailments preventable? Can this be reversed? Humans have the potential, so can they get back to normalcy one day? And, will they get back to normalcy anytime soon, if left to themselves? It doesn't seem so. No human society in the past, so far, has deliberately and consciously altered their societal system to fix its problems. It is time that we try to find a solution for this, if there is one, and hasten the attainment of prosperity, peace, and happiness for all.

If so, how to go about finding the solution that establishes a prosperous, peaceful, happy, and sustainable civilization?

The problem needs to be analyzed methodically and thoroughly before accepting any solution.

CHAPTER 3

Human Behavior and Human Societies—Basic Concepts

HUMAN BEHAVIOR, HUMAN NEEDS, AND ECONOMIC SECURITY

SURVIVAL AND *PROCREATION* OR REPRODUCTION are the fundamental properties of all living beings in a normal ecosystem. That is, under a natural ecosystem, living beings have the ability to survive and produce offspring. This ability is referred to as *biological fitness*. Living beings also have the ability to evolve. Evolution is so directed that their biological fitness gets maximized over time.

Living beings belonging to the *animal kingdom*, including humans, exhibit *physical movements* or *actions or behaviors* for survival and procreation. Behaviors have two components—*innate behavior* and *learned behavior*. Innate behavior is in-built behavior. It is inborn, instinctual, genetically determined, and, therefore, fixed. It is the same in all normal people. Whereas learned behavior, also called *conditioned behavior*, is acquired after birth and is an adaptive mechanism to the changing environment. It is conditioned by the environment that an individual is exposed to. Therefore, it just reflects the type of environment that one is exposed to. In other words, it varies from individual to individual, depending on one's exposure to a particular environment. Learned behavior of even an individual can change over time when there is a change in the environment. Even short-term changes can alter the learned behavior of an individual. Thus, learned behavior is not fixed, unlike innate behavior.

(Note that the terms describing types of behavior are not yet standardized. "Human innate behavior" and "human learned behavior," for example, are referred to by many as "human nature" and "human behavior," respectively.)

Like other animals, human beings have several *economic needs* that they are required to satisfy for their survival. They meet these needs employing their behavior that can be called *economic behavior.* Water, food, shelter, clothing, transportation, protection, healthcare, education, information, and entertainment are basic (material and nonmaterial) needs, which also include healthy local, regional, and global ecosystems. (Note that humans, like other living beings, cannot live isolated from the ecosystem, which is, therefore, a normal and indispensable part of human needs. This need is often overlooked.) Humans are required to satisfy their needs that arise both immediately (short-term) and in the foreseeable future (long-term).

When humans are in a surrounding with a stable availability of resources for satisfying both their short-term and long-term needs, they are said to be in a state called *economic security.* When resources are scarce, humans are in a state of *economic insecurity.* Human economic behavior is such that it seeks economic security and avoids economic insecurity. Thus, when the surrounding economic conditions are favorable, humans are at peace with themselves and are under stress when economic conditions are adverse. Humans have the capacity to adapt to the surrounding economic conditions using their learned behavior to maximize the satisfaction of needs.

HUMAN SOCIETIES, HUMAN SOCIAL BEHAVIOR, ORGANIZATION OF HUMAN SOCIETIES, AND ECONOMIC SYSTEM

Since it is easier to meet one's needs by group living than by solitary living, humans, like many other animals, have evolved into *social beings* or living in groups or societies. The economic advantages of social grouping are due to those of *large-scale operation* or *economies of scale.* Larger the size of a society more would be the *cost-effectiveness* or benefit-cost ratio for each member of the society, where a *benefit* is the amounts of satisfaction of needs. The *cost* includes consumed quantities of material resources, time, and labor or effort. *Economies of scale* is the most fundamental economic principle that is often not emphasized. It is not a much-considered part of the equation of science of social grouping.

Larger the scale of operation, 1) more would be the scope for employing division of labor, specialization, advanced technology (such as mechanization and automation) and 2) less will be both the requirement and wastages of labor or workforce, time, and material.

Put another way, humans, like many other animals, did not evolve into social beings for nothing. They evolved so for economic reasons. Thus, *social groups or societies are nothing but economic groups.*

Humans are, in fact, the most social among all social animals. Being a social animal is evolutionarily determined. That is, humans are genetically designed to be social. Therefore, humans' fundamental nature is *being-social,* unless, of course, affected by mental illnesses associated with aberrant social behavior. Innate behaviors that also come along with being a social animal are being cooperative, helpful, compassionate, gregarious, and fun-loving with fellow humans, all of which maximize the biological fitness of both the group and its individual members. If we find ourselves behaving in any other way, it is only under undue duress such as economic or physical threats, which compel us into doing something against our basic nature or better judgment.

Primitive human societies on earth existed as small groups or bands. At present, humans live in hundreds of politically independent groups/societies called "countries" or "nations" (sovereign nations), each of which has millions of people (citizens) as its members.

To be functional, a modern economic group, which is as big as a nation, requires:

1) *Wealth* or *resources,* 2) *work* or *labor,* and 3) *a central decision-making body.*

1. **Wealth or Resources** means all that are used to satisfy people's needs, namely, a) the *natural resources* and b) *means of production and distribution of goods and services.* Thus wealth includes the *natural resources* (such as land, forests, mines, oceans, and a healthy or balanced ecology) from which useful goods are extracted; the *industries* in which this natural wealth is processed; the *distribution* of that wealth via *transportation networks* (such as roads and truck lines), *distribution centers* (such as grocery and department stores); and *facilities* for providing services (such as schools and hospitals).

2. ***Work or Labor*** is required from people to run the units of production, distribution, and service provision. As a matter of fact, work is needed to provide or satisfy any kind of need.

3. ***A Central Decision-Making Body*** (or loosely called *leadership*) is required for deciding on and coordinating the actions of different components of the society while satisfying the economic needs of the individuals and the society as a whole. The decision-making body consists of one or more members of the society.

The system of society or *societal organization is nothing but the economic system of society* because societies are nothing but *economic groups*. The *economic system*, thus, refers to the way the economy is organized about the systems of ownership of the wealth of the society, satisfying the needs of the members of the society, labor, the structure of the decision-making body, and the way the decision-making body is selected. At present, the economic systems of countries all over the world differ from each other to varying extents.

CHAPTER 4

Economic History of Human Beings

NO SOCIETY SO FAR IN history has deliberately and consciously changed its culture to achieve social betterment. The real reasons behind social changes have been *historical accidents*—natural or economic events that immediately affected large numbers of people.

The way we live is mostly due to historical accidents. So what if we thought it through correctly?

Human species originated over two hundred thousand years ago, and it originated, like any other living species, from common ancestors. It is now well established that humans originated as a single group on Earth at a single geographic location in Africa. This group, therefore, was the ancestor of all human beings on Earth today. (Note, however, that about 85% of modern humans inherited genes solely from the species *Homo sapiens* and the rest inherited up to 5% of genes also from several other species, mainly, *Neanderthal* and *Denisovan*.) During those times, all resources were available freely and directly from nature. Humans, like other social animals, were sharing their work, mainly food-gathering and defense; they also shared the food they gathered according to the individual needs. Humans were economically secure those times because their needs were satisfied freely and directly from natural resources. At that time, there was no question of possession or ownership of any resource such as an object, land or territory, or water sources among humans. At that stage, the human group might not have required a *central decision-making body* or leadership because the group and the roles of group members were simple.

Over time, because of population growth, scarcity of food, geographical changes, natural calamities, or a combination of these, the human species, which was a single group on the whole planet at one time, got divided and subdivided into many separate independent groups and got spread all over Earth. At that time, primitive human societies existed as small groups or bands, lived as *hunter-gatherers,* and were mostly nomadic. Having separated, these groups lost contact and communication with each other and, as a result, also lost acquaintance with each other. Due to this *estrangement,* each group might have considered humans of other groups as creatures of another species. It was here only that the first tendencies of *ownership* or *"ours-theirs" possessiveness* were born in humans. Possessiveness is when you want to have something and don't want to share it with others. It is mainly the result of *economic insecurity* due to scarcity or threat of impending scarcity, real or perceived. Due to this, these primitive human groups were at war with other groups to own or possess the food, territory, and other natural resources. This development was the first *milestone* in the deviation of the human economy toward the economy found in modern societies.

Nevertheless, despite the frictions between these groups, there was toleration and cooperation within the group; all needs were still obtained freely from nature; all members of the group were still sharing their work according to individual ability and sharing the food according to the individual needs; there was still no individual ownership of any object or territory within the group. At this stage, the human groups might have required a *central decision-making body* or leadership, mainly because of the wars fought with other groups. The physically stronger males needed to be fighting the war and be the decision-makers or the group leaders. This development must be when the need for societies to be male-dominated first arose.

Then *agriculture* started in human societies some twelve thousand years ago. The advent of agriculture and later *animal farming* led the nomadic human communities to change into settled ones. Now, human tribes had more to *own* or *possess* and to *fight* for—inhabitable and arable land, water source, and farm animals. Agriculture was thus the next milestone toward the evolution of the economy into the modern one. This stage, the feudal era, was the worst phase in human civilization—a few warlords owned most of the wealth and acted as masters treating the rest, the vast majority, as slaves. Later, these warring groups must have realized, while still estranged, that the company of other groups was unavoidable and that war brings loss of life and properties. And soon they learned, to their benefit, while being still estranged, to tolerate *trade by barter* with other groups. The birth of trade, it can be said, was the next important step toward the present-day economy. Later, trade by barter got evolved into a more expedient and refined system with the introduction of *money* or *currency as a medium of exchange.*

Warlords and kings were the *central decision-making body.* Males, being physically stronger, were invariably the decision-makers or leaders. Thus, at first, it was an authoritarian or dictatorial regime all over the world taking care of central decision-making. Another relatively recent milestone in the evolution of the present-day economy is *industrialization* involving the large-scale production of goods of needs. Human tribes transformed into bigger and more complex groups called countries or nation. A couple of centuries ago, dictatorship gave way to democracy as the central decision-making system, which is now the case in most countries. With the advent of democracy, human civilization recovered a bit—the master-slave human relation changed a bit into an owner-worker one.

This economic system that has been there all over the world has been named as *capitalism* or *market economy* since a couple of centuries ago. Capitalism is the economic system that now exists in all the nations of the world.

Along with this evolution and growth of capitalism, there was also an intensification of human estrangement and possessiveness. The estrangement that was there between groups to start with has now infiltrated into the groups and between individuals. *Ours-theirs* possessiveness gave way to *mine-others* possessiveness. The advent of full-fledged capitalism meant each individual bearing one's economic responsibilities. Thus capitalism got known to be an *individualistic economic system.*

Society, at present, mainly consists of the *owner class* and the *working class.* The owner class is a small minority, and the working class is a vast majority. It is estimated that less than 10 percent of the people own more than 90 percent of the world's wealth. Note that though the work of the working class alone produces the wealth of the society, the owner class holds most of its wealth.

In summary, the human species was a single socialistic group, to begin with, in the remote past. It then got divided, subdivided, and so on into separate groups because of the scarcity of food, population explosion, or natural calamities. This separation brought estrangement between groups. The groups were possessive and at war with other groups to possess food, territory, and other natural resources. This possessiveness was the first step toward the present capitalism. The advent of agriculture about twelve thousand years ago, with the accompanying requirement of land and water source, made humans further possessive and warring. Later with the advent of trade, currency, and industrialization, it gave way to the present economic system—capitalism or market economy—which is less warring, less uncivilized, more tolerating, and sophisticated. However, with capitalism, which is an individualistic economy, human estrangement and possessiveness have spread to the individual level.

Moreover, at present, most of the society's wealth is owned by a small minority—the owner class, which gets its wealth produced by the work of the rest—the working class, which is a vast majority. The central decision-making body was dictatorial for a long time, and now it is democracy in most of the countries.

Thus, the roots of the capitalist economy evolved naturally since prehistoric times out of historical accidents. It is not that one day a group of wise folks from different parts of the world sat together, thought through, conceived, and adopted this system.

CHAPTER 5

Features of Capitalism

THE SINGLE FUNDAMENTAL FEATURE OF the capitalistic economic system is *individual* or *private ownership* of society's wealth. All other elements of capitalism are the consequence of or originate from or centered on this fundamental feature, namely, private ownership of wealth or property. Capitalism, therefore, may rightly be called *private ownership based economy*.

PRIVATE OWNERSHIP AND INHERITANCE OF WEALTH

Each individual is allowed to *own* or *possess* private wealth or property. This feature means that the individual has the full right to use their wealth in the manner they like to use to satisfy their own needs.

Ownership of wealth is usually *inherited* from the parents to children.

Thus, the wealth of society exists divided among individuals. Wealth, in the present capitalistic system, by the way, is not owned equally among the people. Under this system, the means of production and distribution are monopolized by a small capitalist class. That is, a small minority of people—the *owner class* or the rich class—possess most of the wealth, and the rest are the working class or the poor class.

TRADE AND MONETARY SYSTEM

The needs of people are provided and obtained by *trade*. People sell their goods, services, and labor for buying goods, services, and labor they need from others. They follow the *monetary system* for trading; that is, they use *money* as a medium of exchange.

The production and distribution of goods and services are by *businesspeople* or *private entrepreneurs* who live off the *profits* they obtain by selling goods and services they produce and distribute. They also reinvest their profits to make more wealth. In an average nation, there are millions of independent private entrepreneurs.

In other words, everyone in the capitalist model is engaged in some form of trade to make a living, whether it is trading labor for a wage or selling a product for profit. Profit, which the private entrepreneurs make, is, in fact, the surplus-value of the labor that the workers put up.

STATE OR GOVERNMENT

"State" or the "government" is the administrative institution, which also comprises the central decision-making body or the legislature. The decision-making body is democratically elected in the majority of countries. In some countries, it is run by a dictatorship. The government also runs at least some essential services such as military, police, justice, and so on, and cannot afford to leave them to private enterprise. The taxes collected from people run the government.

FAMILY OR HOUSEHOLD AS THE CONSUMER UNIT

Every family or household, having one to several people as members, is a private and independent *consumer unit* residing in a *house* or *domicile* having facilities for mainly shelter, food, and protection.

Economic Classes — Owners, Workers, and the Jobless

A society is composed primarily of two classes of people—the *owners* and the *nonowners.*

Owners are the ones who own wealth, which includes money. They are a small minority in society though they own most of its wealth. They are the *wealthy class.* The rest of the people or people other than owners or the nonowners who are the vast majority are the *poor class.* Many of the owners are *self-employed* or *businesspeople* or *private entrepreneurs* and many of them act as *employers* under whom many more work as *workers* or *employees.* There are also *government employees* working in government institutions. Some of the owners and the workers belong, economically, to the *middle class.* There are also the jobless or the unemployed who belong to the *poor class.*

The self-employed live by the *profit* they make from their private enterprise or business, and the *workers* or *employees,* private or government, live by the *salary* or *wages* they get for their work from the private entrepreneurs or the government.

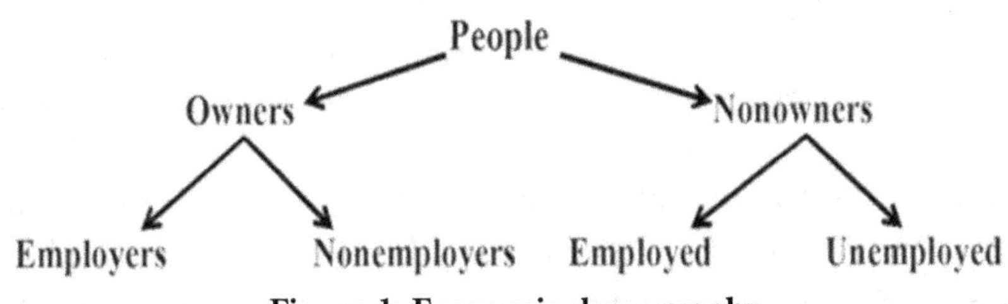

Figure 1: Economic demography

CHAPTER 6

Capitalism and the Prevailing Human Ailments

IF ONE OBSERVES THE PRESENT-DAY social and individual ills and analyzes them a bit, it can be inferred that the root cause of all human ills is the *economic scarcity* and its effect—*economic insecurity*, at the social and individual levels. Economic insecurity has been the sole fear haunting nations, economic institutions, small as well as big, families, and even the individuals of the owner or the wealthy class. Since the economic status or prosperity of a society or a nation, that is, of its people, depends mainly upon the adopted economic system, one can safely presume that the cause of this economic insecurity is the disorder or the defects in the present economic system. That is to say that capitalism or the market economy, which has been with us for quite a long time, has been the root cause of economic insecurity and hence for all social ills. Capitalism has been found to be unscientific and, therefore, inefficient. The system is also unfair to the working-class people who constitute the most majority. These faults are not anomalies of the system—but represent a natural, though accidental, evolution of capitalism over time.

Thus capitalism is not only inefficient but harmful to the interests of human beings. It is not favorable for realizing prosperity, peace, and happiness, or attaining the peak of human civilization.

The details explaining the defects of capitalism and how they cause the prevailing human problems are dealt in the next chapter.

CHAPTER 7

Defects of Capitalism as an Economic System and How That Causes the Prevailing Human Problems

CAPITALIST ECONOMIC SYSTEM EXISTS AS MULTIPLE SMALL UNITS—AN EXTREMELY UNECONOMICAL SYSTEM

THE MOST FUNDAMENTAL PRINCIPLE OF economics is *economies of scale—larger the scale of operation more is the cost-effectiveness* (benefit-cost ratio) *for each member of the group.* Smaller the scale of operation, therefore, less would be the benefits because: 1) less would be the scope for employing division of labor, specialization, and advanced technology, such as mechanization and automation and 2) more will be both the requirement and wastages of workforce, time, and materials. Therefore, there would be less production and more wastes of time, labor, and personnel. This principle holds good at all levels of scale—a household, an organization, an industry, a nation, or even a possible future world society.

The capitalist economy is individualistic and exists as multiple or millions of small units or economic holdings. Therefore, the benefits of large-scale operation are minimal, which is the direct consequence of this drawback of capitalism. For this reason, capitalism is unscientific and, so, inefficient in a purely economic sense. That is, this system enormously diminishes both human prosperity and leisure because of the slower rate of production of goods or provision of service and requirement of more material resources and workforce.

Material scarcity, as opposed to material abundance, is thus the primary hallmark of capitalism.

This inefficiency is the main drawback of capitalism as an economic system.

PLANNING, CONTROL, AND COORDINATION OF THE ECONOMY

Because of its existence as multiple independent units, the capitalist economy imposes constraints on economic planning, control, and coordination between the various units. These constraints lead to uncoordinated economic decisions that result in a tremendous waste of material resources, time, and labor. A lack of coordination produces a vast and wasteful multiplicity in material and labor along with problematic incompatibility between the same type of structural components of goods produced by different producers.

In other words, operational efficiency is low in capitalism. Thus, this is yet another reason why capitalism is an unscientific, inefficient, and wasteful economic system.

PROFIT MOTIVE AND ITS ILL EFFECTS

Because private wealth acquisition is the basis of the capitalist system, the object of creating goods and services would be to sell them profitably. Therefore, the production of commodities would be based upon the producers' expectation of making a profit and not according to the needs of the society. Thus they invariably tend to increase the profit from their business, and there is little control by the society or government to prevent this profit motive from becoming unscrupulous and greedy. Several methods are employed to enhance the profit—reducing the investment, inflating the prices of goods and services, creating a scarcity of goods, creating artificial needs in people by advertisement, keeping the quality of goods and services low, not repairing and recycling of goods, or a combination of these.

When commodities are scarce, prices increase. Scarcity is artificially created by decreasing the production or even destroying the goods to improve the demand and, thus, also the price. Capitalistic logic means that if goods cannot be sold at a profit, they are either not produced at all or destroyed. Capitalism, as an economy, requires a high degree of scarcity. Goods such as food items are many times destroyed to keep prices high. We are living with the contradiction—millions are starving, and food is regularly destroyed to keep their prices high.

For the same reasons, to jack up the sales of newly manufactured goods, the repair and recycling of goods are not encouraged. Products are wasted by use-and-throw culture.

Consumption drives capitalism. Advertising industries brainwash people to create artificial needs in them whether it improves their lives or not (*consumerism*), thus increasing consumption and profit. The advertisement has been successful even in creating a *value system disorder* in people. Possessing expensive branded items, for example, has become a symbol of high status.

The reduction of investment compromises the quality of goods and services. Also, the quality of goods and services is deliberately kept low not only to save on investment but to reduce the durability of goods or benefits of services so that consumption and profit are increased.

Thus there are wastes of overproduction of goods and services, production of low-quality goods and services, wastes of advertisement, and the accompanying excess labor and development of an unhealthy habit of frenzy consumerism among people.

Furthermore, because of profit-seeking, money has taken on a life of its own. Money, which replaced the trade-by-barter system as just a more expedient and convenient "medium of exchange," has evolved into its present unreal, inhuman form. The basis of the current economy is not the creation of goods and service, or labor that provides human needs but merely a profit. That is, if there is enough money, it alone can make more money—"money makes money." Consider the financial institutions like banks and stock exchange, for instance. Banks earn interest on loans given; the value of stock exchange is decided just by speculation by the masses. This "money-making-money" phenomenon has led to environmental, public health, and other humanitarian issues that are considered irrelevant and "external" in the equation of economy.

Worst, however, is the case of profit motive becoming unscrupulous, greedy, and unethical. Here are such instances from the health sector, for example. What about drug and food companies funding and corrupting the medical research to get a research conclusion favorable for the consumption of their products? ("In Asia's Fattest Country, Nutritionists Take Money from Food Giants—*New York Times*, December 2017). Where is the doctor's integrity when they prescribe medication because of the revenue the doctor will generate based on a contract agreement with its pharmaceutical company?

Capitalism, with its drive to make profits, brings about endless problems. This drive for profit is the root cause of many more ills, as explained in the following sections.

UNEMPLOYMENT, UNDEREMPLOYMENT, AND MISEMPLOYMENT

Paradoxically, gross *unemployment, underemployment* or low-paying jobs, and *misemployment* are bound to exist in capitalism despite having enough wealth and technology in society. That is because companies tend to become bigger and bigger to get the benefits of the cost-effectiveness of the large-scale operation. Larger the scale of operation, lesser the workforce required. Another reason for unemployment is the use of technologies such as machines, automation, robotics, and artificial intelligence, which reduce the need for labor. This issue is the structural contradiction of capitalism. Under capitalism, humanity cannot get the full benefit of machines, automation, robotics, artificial intelligence, and so on because it leads to unemployment. Another reason for unemployment is the profit motive. Employers tend to employ fewer employees, extract maximum labor from them, and pay them just enough to meet their most basic needs just for subsistence. Put another way, given the technology and long work hours, there is not enough work in this world to engage everyone.

CAPITALISM, ECONOMIC INSECURITY, AND SOCIAL BEHAVIOR

Capitalism requires competition among people, which is bound to affect adversely on human social behavior.

Genetics determines the characteristics of the body, such as the color of the eyes and shape of the nose. But it has nothing to do with learned social behaviors of a person, such as selfishness or greediness.

As opposed to innate human behavior, learned or conditioned human behavior is an adaptive mechanism to the changing environment. Learned behavior is acquired from the surrounding by way of learning once a person is born. Most of what people refer to as "innate human behavior" or "innate human nature" is learned behavior of people, which is just an effect of the conditions around them. That is, the learned human behavior is not fixed. Humans behave differently depending on the conditions they live in.

Human economic behavior is such that it seeks economic security and avoids economic insecurity. Humans can adapt to the surrounding economic conditions by their learned behavior to maximize the satisfaction of their needs.

Humans are the most social among all social animals. Being a social animal is evolutionally determined. Therefore, as pointed out in an earlier section, humans are genetically designed to be social. So, humans' basic nature is *being-social,* unless, of course, affected by mental illnesses associated with aberrant social behavior. Innate behaviors that come with being a social animal are being cooperative, helpful, compassionate, gregarious, and fun-loving with fellow humans. If we find ourselves behaving in any other way, it is only under undue duress such as economic or physical threats, constraints, and so on from natural or human-made causes that compel us into doing something against our basic nature or better judgment.

Human social behavior, therefore, reflects the society people live in. Social behavior is a conditioned behavior acquired from the surrounding society. Put in other words, the social behavior of an individual depends on the system of the society he or she has been living in.

Like many other animals, humans evolved into social beings for economic reasons. Therefore, societies are nothing but *economic groups* and the *system of society* is nothing but the *economic system* of society. Thus, the *economic systems* of the societies, past and present, shape the human social behavior.

Capitalism is an economy based on private ownership. It is an individualistic economy that requires people to spend their private wealth to meet their needs. The total wealth in a society is limited, and scarcity and unemployment are hallmarks of capitalism. Further, in a capitalist society, people can lose profits or their jobs, or their careers are threatened by other workers, or fall sick, or grow old. Furthermore, few people can be sure of continued employment. In many cases, one cannot be sure that the type of work they have been trained in will be in demand next year. All these make people feel economically insecure. Thus *economic insecurity* is yet another hallmark of capitalism. Because of economic uncertainty, people tend to acquire and accumulate wealth aggressively as possession provides some security. People have reasons to worry about tomorrow, and they need a cushion of wealth to fall back on. The capitalistic condition has nurtured intense competition over cooperation among people for the acquisition of wealth or even just survival.

Because of economic insecurity, a human being who is a born social being and who, at the origin of human species, had a social behavior of *cooperation* and *mutual compassion,* has been taken over by *possessiveness* and *mutual rivalry.* The capitalist economy has made society a fertile breeding ground for the growth of maladaptive, counterproductive social behaviors—greed, mutual distrust, envy, aggression, paranoia, divisiveness, and hatred among people.

Humans are now a divided lot though they belong to the same animal species, and even though their ancestors are common. They are separated by economic class, gender, race, nationality, language, region, religion, caste, and so on.

Also, for the same reasons, capitalism brings about a distorted value system, priorities, preferences, and attitudes in people. The idea of becoming rich, powerful, and famous, by whatever means necessary, has been a life-guiding force. One's possessed wealth determines the assessment of one's social status and self-esteem, and also the extent of egoistic tendency. In this money-based society, the more possessions people achieve, the more value they have. The idea of money, wealth, work, and so on has been conditioning our minds for a long time, making us prisoners to a system that puts us under the sway of illusions of security, power, freedom, social status, and so on. The measure of success has been the acquisition of wealth, power, and fame rather than the fulfillment of one's pursuits.

EFFECT OF CAPITALISM ON DEMOCRACY

Let us never forget that government is ourselves and
not an alien power over us. The ultimate rulers of our
democracy are not a President and senators, congressmen
and government officials, but the voters of this country.

—FRANKLIN D. ROOSEVELT

Democracy is peculiar to human species. Democracy, as opposed to dictatorship, is the single most crucial milestone in the evolution of the decision- or policy-making system or the political system of human societies.

Democracy is a form of government wherein the supreme power of decision-making is in the hands of the people. Democracy is based on the assumption that every member of a society has a stake in how the society is organized and run, and therefore, everybody will have the right to participate in the social decisions that affect them. By providing equal voting rights, democracy ensures that even the ordinary citizens have decision-making power equal to that of even the rich and the powerful.

Additional advantages of democracy are as follows:

1. People feel a sense of fairness in the social decisions that are made democratically, even if some decisions are against their liking. On the contrary, people feel frustrated under dictatorship when the decisions made are not to their liking. Therefore, popular revolt is a common phenomenon under the dictatorship but not in a democracy. By way of elections, democracy can offer modifications in government without people having to resort to hostility or violence.

2. Democracy permits all, including the common public, to play an active part in society's political actions. They get the chance to speak their views through voting for selecting their government. Thereby citizens achieve a sense of contribution to society.

3. Democracy ensures that the elected representatives in power function effectively for their people; otherwise,

they might not elect them in subsequent elections. This mechanism averts the monopoly of the reigning representatives.

4. Democracy ensures transparency in governance, and, free speech and debate among people and independent media.

5. Further, political candidates tend to compete with each other in crystallizing the opinions of ordinary people on public issues that affect their lives and policies that tackle such issues.

6. All these elements of democracy gradually ensure enhanced public education and awareness especially on public and political issues.

However, the existing democracies all over the world need much to be reformed. (See "Ultimate Reforms in Democracy under the Existing Capitalism" in a later section of this book.)

One of the glaring defects in the existing system is that the legislative or political talent of the poor is not available for the society's service because only the rich can afford the exorbitant election campaign expenses.

Moreover, democratic reforms take place at a rather slow pace mainly because capitalism resists any change, only to perpetuate the hold of capitalists on the political system

Why is the capitalist class reluctant to allow any *reform in democracy?*

In capitalism, because of the rat race for the acquisition of wealth, the government would often become corrupt. Majority of laws are made favoring corporates, which persuade, lobby, or bribe the government to make laws in their interests. Political parties of all types claim to be working for the betterment of society but pass laws that take care of the profit interests of the big business owners or capitalists as a group.

Capitalism can be administered in the only way it can be done—in the interests of the capitalist class. Political parties and hence the State, under capitalism, more or less act like a mere extension of the corporate executive. For these reasons, a "democracy" of a capitalist nation is, in reality, *a dictatorship of the capitalists* or *corporate oligarchy.*

This unethical nexus between the capitalists and the government, called crony capitalism, makes the government ineffective for society's real issues. The essential services like education, health care, development, law and order, and so on, which are under the government purview are neglected. That would hinder society's progress, besides creating other direct problems.

> *Modern politics is business politics. That is true both*
> *of foreign and domestic policy. Legislation, police*
> *surveillance, the administration of justice, the military and*
> *diplomatic service, all are chiefly concerned with business*
> *relations, pecuniary interests, and they have little more*
> *than an incidental bearing on other human interests.*

> — THORSTEIN VEBLEN, ECONOMIST AND
> SOCIOLOGIST (1857–1929)

ECONOMIC INEQUALITY AND CLASS STRUGGLE IN CAPITALISM

Larger the scale of operation more would be the cost-effectiveness. Therefore, big businesses and industries can produce goods and services at cheaper rates than smaller ones. That is, smaller players cannot compete with the bigger ones. Thus in capitalism, the scope for earning wealth is more for those who are already wealthy—*money makes money*. Therefore, the wealth of a society tends to get concentrated in the hands of very few people, and the wealth gap between the very rich and the rest continues to grow. In 2010, the wealthiest forty-three people owned 50 percent of the world's wealth, but in 2017, just the eight wealthiest individuals held the same percentage of the world's wealth. The richest 1 percent took home 82 percent of the wealth generated around the globe in 2017 (Oxfam study). *Inheritance of wealth* that is there in this system also favors the concentration of wealth. In other words, despite a country having enough wealth, because of capitalism, this wealth does not reach the majority of people who are bound to remain poor. Because of these economic inequalities and also because of unemployment, there would appear, in this system, basically two economic classes, namely, 1) the owner class or the rich class and 2) the rest, the working class or the poor class. This economic inequality is inherent and inevitable in capitalism. Even though some workers own shares, they do not have the luxury to quit their jobs.

The economic inequality would always produce antagonism or class wars between these two classes. It is not a matter of good and evil people. The different interests of the classes cause the antagonism. Some capitalists may be nice on a personal level, but they will always have interests different from the working class. It is the logic of the capitalist economic system.

Manifestations of this antagonism are theft, robbery, riots, armed insurgency, terrorism, and war (at the international level). Anger is a product of deprivation—real, relative, or perceived. Some external factor is often blamed as the source for the expression of anger.

Social instability caused by excessive disparities in income distribution, in addition, requires corrective measures in the form of social welfare policies for the poor (minimum wages, free education and healthcare, unemployment insurance, and so on). The cost of these measures needs to be met by taxing profits of the rich, which, in turn, gives rise to dishonesty and likelihood of tax evasion by the rich. This social instability cripples capitalism and its incentive system, and also, incurs high administrative costs.

The wealth of the society was already owned by those who were there before you. For what fault does one get born to the poor? This unanswerable moral question exemplifies the economic unjustness inherent in capitalism. This unjust system not only leads to inhuman conditions for the vast majority but is a source of justification for crimes by the economically deprived class. "Economic inequality undermines human rights" says a UN expert in a March 2016 report.

Is the issue of 'economic equality' the most basic human right?

PERIODIC RECESSION IS PART OF A CAPITALIST ECONOMY

The capitalist or market economy is plagued by recurrent recession wherein the economy collapses and comes to a standstill—with inflated prices for goods and services, losses for companies, job layoffs, and so on. Recession is periodic or cyclic. Consumption drives the capitalist economy. Anything that brings down consumption, therefore, contributes to slowing down the economy. The causes of recession are the contradicting factors that are inherent in the capitalist economy. Profit motive leads to a hike in the prices of goods, and so, consumers cannot afford to purchase the same. The profit motive also leads to the overproduction of commodities. The fundamental criterion for economic activity in capitalism is the accumulation of capital for reinvestment in production. Accumulation of capital spurs the development of new, nonproductive industries, such as the financial industry, that only exist to help the accumulation process continue (otherwise, the system goes into crisis). Another cause for recession is job lay-offs as a consequence of new technologies like automation, which reduces the need for human labor and thus increases unemployment. However, if people are unemployed, consumption comes down, and the economy collapses. These factors, along with people's behavior of money-saving, bring the economy to a standstill. As long as profit is the ultimate motive, the recession will persist with the same cycle of events.

Recurrence of recession is a sure sign that capitalism, as an economic system, does not just work and is ill-suited for the society.

CAPITALISM IS BURDENED WITH WASTES AND COSTS OF CURRENCY, BANKING, TAX SYSTEM, INSURANCE, ADVERTISEMENT, POLICE, JUDICIARY, AND MILITARY

Capitalism is a trade- or market-based economy. Therefore, the usage of money or currency (medium of exchange), banking, tax system, and insurance is inevitable.

In capitalism, advertisement is required for a private enterprise to boost their sales. Besides, since capitalism breeds crime, there are also wastes and costs of police and judiciary for the maintenance of law and order. Further, since capitalism is the cause of international economic insecurity, international war is bound to occur periodically. Therefore, the use of the military, and arms production and purchase are unavoidable.

Thus, currency, banking, tax system, insurance, advertisement, police, judiciary, and military are required in a society only due to the economic system—capitalism. All these result in unnecessary costs and wastes of materials, labor, and time, and other hardships like human suffering.

CAPITALISM AND ECOLOGICAL IMBALANCE

Global warming is real and happening. Earth's 2016 surface temperatures were the warmest since modern recordkeeping began in 1880. 2016 was the third year in a row to set a new record for global average surface temperatures. 2017 was the second-hottest year on record and was the hottest year without the short-term warming influence of an El Nino event. The 10 warmest years in the 138-year record all have occurred since 2000.

—NASA/NOAA

Human life, like that of other living beings, is part of the ecosystem. It cannot develop or survive apart from a healthy ecosystem. The world is facing an acute ecological crisis, which has caused several major global problems: global warming, rising sea levels, ozone depletion, acid rain, water shortages, soil degradation, environmental pollution, loss of biodiversity, extinction of species, and so on. All these issues are a threat to human development and survival. Now there is a consensus that unsustainable human actions have destroyed the ecosystem over the last two hundred years or so since the start of industrialization.

"Scientists Agree: Global Warming is Happening and Humans are the Primary Cause" (Union of Concerned Scientists, Aug 2018).

Some of the main unsustainable human actions causing ecological imbalance are the use of fossil fuel, deforestation, industrial wastes, overpopulation, use of plastic, and the use of agricultural pesticides. There is also the awareness that the root cause of these ecologically unsustainable human activities is the greed-driven suicide machine—the capitalist system. The capitalist's pursuit of wealth accumulation is limitless. The Earth is being plundered, and the environment ransacked for profit. Further, it isn't easy to plan, control, and coordinate the capitalist economy. Each person can do anything for one's interests—trade expansion and resource acquisition. Also, the government cannot stop this destruction as it has to pass laws that maintain profits for the industries. Otherwise, the capitalist economy will nosedive. Both the United States and Russia are rejecting the idea that human activities are the cause of global warming—obviously because both countries economically rely heavily on the business of fossil fuel. The governments need to protect the business. Further, there is hardly any international control to prevent any country from accumulating wealth even if it is at the expense of ecology.

The planet'll shake us off like a bad case of fleas.

—George Carlin, on the ecological crisis

"UN's Solution to Climate Change: End Capitalism" (Oct 2018)
"To Save Ourselves It's Time to Rethink Our Economic System. The Market is Killing the Planet. Warn Scientists" (Science Alert, Sep 2018).

The picture looks gloomy, but there are silver linings. Consider the following relatively recent developments on global ecology.

1) The hole in the Ozone layer has shrunk thanks to the ban of chlorofluorocarbons (CFCs). It may be a direct result of the Montreal Protocol, which was signed by all countries of the world in 1985 to phase out CFCs.

2) Today, almost 100% of the electricity consumed in Iceland comes from renewable energy—80% geothermal and 20% hydroelectric. The story of Iceland's transition from fossil fuels may inspire other countries seeking to increase their share of renewable energy. Currently, to be sure, over 20 countries in the world are producing electricity from geothermal energy. However, its contribution to the overall electricity requirement is meager.

3) In July 2018, Ireland became the world's first country to move to divest from fossil fuels, a development that marks the most significant advance to date for a divestment campaign pushed by environmentalists worldwide—The Guardian; The New York Times.

CAPITALISM AND DIFFICULTY IN THE UTILIZATION OF AVAILABLE NEWER SCIENTIFIC TECHNOLOGIES

The human potential for inventions in scientific technology is almost limitless. It is a contradiction in capitalism that many of the available newer scientific technologies are not being employed or employed rather slowly. That is because of the inherent nature of capitalism—mainly, profit motive and the existing extent of unemployment.

We already have the technology to meet the basic needs of all people sustainably. Now we can produce, for example, enough of sustainable, renewable, and clean energy. Electricity can now be generated in enough quantities from solar energy, wind, waves, heat concentrators, geothermal energy, and so on to entirely do away with fossil fuels and nuclear reactors that are damaging our ecosystem.

To solve the food shortage, we have developed enough food production technologies—hydroponic farms, aquaculture, vertical farming, ocean farming, and so on.

We have made considerable advances in areas like mechanization, 3-D printing technology, maglev transportation (that requires minimal energy, attains high speed, and is safe), self-driven vehicles (that is accident-free), information technology, automation, robotics, artificial intelligence, nanotechnology, and biotechnology to enhance production sustainably and reduce human labor requirements to a bare minimum.

Why are these newer, more beneficial technologies not implemented?

Some of the reasons are: change and progress are met with resistance in the capitalist system as they often bring down the profits of established institutions; corporate owners of older technologies lobby and bribe the governments to prevent or slow down the utilization of newer technologies; starting newer technologies involves high investments and making substantial profits takes time; implementing newer technologies involves loss of jobs.

Commercialization of Education, Healthcare, Entertainment, and Art in Capitalism

Education, healthcare, entertainment, and art are the prime areas that determine the quality of life. In capitalism, because of the profit motive, these fields have got commercialized, and hence their qualities compromised.

Workplace Satisfaction under Capitalism

Given the rate of unemployment, underemployment, and misemployment, capitalism has become an "earn a living or suffer" system. Most employees are slaves to the job they don't like, knowing well that earning money is mandatory and also that they can lose the job at any moment. The workplace experience of most people is like working in a private dictatorship under the control of superiors—a top-down, hierarchical dictatorship. That is not surprising. The employers have to control the employees who are bound to be reluctant to work sincerely because of the exploitative practices of the former, such as, prolonged work hours and meager pay scale. At the end of a workday, employees return home feeling defeated and tired. A vast majority of them spend most of their life working and sleeping. For most, a sense of accomplishment is not there; occupations are not enjoyed; and over time, many lose motivation. *The Gallup organization* reminds us every couple of years that nearly 70 percent of employees globally are actively disengaged. (March 2018) A survey concludes that most American workers are dissatisfied (*Forbes*, Susan Adams, 2012).

Capitalism and Lack of Leisure

Leisure means having both free time and economic security.

Leisure is a necessity for people as it allows relaxation and the expression of their creativity and individuality. Lack of leisure causes mental stress and would often lead to behavioral disorders.

In capitalism, enormously more work is required than is necessary as the benefits of large-scale operation are minimal. And also, because of the profit motive, employers tend to extract maximum labor time from employees. Besides, given the existing extent of unemployment in society, there is social pressure against mechanization, automation, use of robotics, and so on. That further prevents the reduction of manual work required. It is yet another contradiction in capitalism that unemployment exists, on the one hand, and the employed are working overtime, on the other.

As a result, many people, especially the middle class, often accumulate financial debt for education, owning vehicles and houses, and so on, spending most of their life working to clear the debt.

Thus, under capitalism, people have been conditioned to consider work as the purpose of their life or even that "work is worship," forgetting that there is more to life than working.

EDUCATIONAL BURDEN ON CHILDREN AND STUDENTS AND ITS EFFECT ON THEIR CREATIVITY UNDER CAPITALISM

Curiosity is an essential aspect of human nature. It drives learning, expression of rationality, creativity, and development of individuality. Children have an insatiable curiosity. If encouraged, they could have a much higher choice of interests and capabilities to develop. Capitalism destroys curiosity instead of harnessing it.

Unemployment and underemployment are inevitable in capitalism. Therefore, there is competition among people to get employed. As a result, school examinations have become more competitive and demanding. At the same time, school syllabi have acquired a vast amount of unnecessary information for students to learn. That is a huge burden for students who are often forced to rote learning. This burden affects them adversely—it suppresses curiosity and, hence, their creativity and individuality.

I have never let my schooling interfere with my education.

—Mark Twain

Capitalism and Superstitions
Needless to say that superstitions are not only useless but wasteful and harmful.

In capitalism, because of poverty and unemployment, people find ways to make wealth by exploiting gullible people through fraud. They commit fraud by deliberately and actively spreading superstitions among people. These include religion, caste, ghosts, miracle, faith healing, astrology, and so on. Fraudsters like priests, exorcists, miracle-men, and astrologers try to spread superstitions for fleecing money from people. Further, since the poor are mostly uneducated, they become easy prey to superstitions. Also, many rich make wealth by exploiting others, which the rich are well aware of. To cover up this guilt of exploitation, they indulge in superstitions, such as religion, and try to exhibit their "virtues", for example, taking undue advantage of the people's misconception that a "god"-fearing person cannot cheat.

Religion is now a multitrillion-dollar racket. Besides, since the rich are keen on conserving capitalism, they try to popularize everything associated with capitalism, including *conservatism* itself, by indulging in and encouraging superstitions. Thus in capitalism, there would always be the paradox of coexistence of both advanced scientific technology and a high rate of superstition. Belief in superstitions misleads people on managing their life and curbs people's natural curiosity, rationality, healthy skepticism, creativity, and development of individuality.

Burdens on the Head of the Family under Capitalism

In capitalism, since each family is an independent economic unit and the government is inefficient, the responsibilities of providing food, shelter, health, education, and employment to all members of the family rest on the head of the family, usually father, mother, husband or wife. This responsibility can be a considerable economic burden and hence, also the cause for mental stress on them.

Capitalism and Laziness

Human beings are born dynamic, curious, and creative. The capitalist system compels people, right from childhood, to be engaged in activities that they don't enjoy. It is this monotonous and boring drudgery that makes people demotivated, hence causing the prevalent "universal laziness."

Children are overburdened in schools with learning excess of information on things that do not have immediate relevance to life. During adulthood, because of unemployment and lack of capital for self-employment, people cannot go after the jobs they are interested in. Because of this, people become demotivated, despite being born-dynamic. Besides, in this system, since the earnings of the employees are not commensurate with the amount of their work and the employees, and even the employers, work for long hours in a day—that is, get less leisure—there would be further loss of interest in the jobs people do. Many "lazy" people are not intrinsically lazy but are so because they have not found what they want to do. People spend their best hours in the job that have become so abstract and specialized that they can no longer fully understand its purpose or contribution in improving other people's lives.

ECONOMIC DEPENDENCE OF WOMEN ON MEN UNDER CAPITALISM

Under capitalism, there is unemployment; women are generally less educated; it is difficult for women to compete for jobs with physically stronger men; women are economically vulnerable during pregnancy; the responsibility of childcare resides mostly with women; society is male-dominated; superstition and conservatism exists. All these reasons ensure that women will be economically dependent upon men. That, by the way, further makes the capitalist society a male-dominated one.

THE INSTITUTION OF MARRIAGE AND SEXUAL DEPRIVATION UNDER CAPITALISM

Heterosexual *marriage* is a social contract of partnership between man and woman for mutual satisfaction of mainly sexual needs and economic needs. Marriages usually have been monogamous—that is, one male would be in a lifelong partnership with one woman. Marriage has social and legal sanctions. The practice of marriage originated and continues to exist because of capitalism. Capitalism causes economic insecurity in people, which is more so for women. Also, women become economically more vulnerable during pregnancy and while bringing up their children. Hence there is social pressure on man, more than on woman, to bear the economic burden of the marriage partnership in return for satisfying his sexual needs. The problem of marriage is that sex outside marriage has become a taboo. So people are generally deprived of mating till marriage and are restricted to mate with a single partner after marriage throughout their lives. That is, because of this system, humans are not only much deprived of sexual pleasure, the highest form of pleasure, but also have lost variety in it. Evolutionally speaking, variety in mating-partners produces genetic diversity in the population. This diversity enhances the biological fitness of the species. Sexual deprivation is part of the reason people lose purpose, motivation, or interest in living. Sexual restrictions also breed other social ills, namely prostitution and sexually transmitted diseases. Poverty and unemployment that originate from capitalism are the other causes of prostitution, and prostitution, in turn, is the primary cause of sexually transmitted diseases. Social restriction due to monogamy denies privacy to unmarried heterosexual couples. This restriction might be very much the cause of homosexuality, which, in turn, can be a source of social disharmony. Other ills of monogamy are marital disharmony, divorce, miseries associated with divorce, especially for women and their children, obsession with sex, sexual perversions, rape, and even drug addiction. Poverty and unemployment, as dealt before, are causes for illicit drug trade and hence also for addiction in capitalism. Besides, the negligence of education, including sex education, in this system further favors the breeding of the above social ills.

FREEDOM FOR WOMEN TO DECIDE ABOUT CHILD CONCEPTION UNDER CAPITALISM

Under capitalism, especially in developing countries, women have less freedom to choose how many children to conceive. They also don't have the choice from whom to conceive their children. This twin issue, which is because of their subordination to men and the institution of marriage, has adverse effects on population control and the biological fitness of humans, as explained in the next sections.

CAPITALISM AND BIOLOGICAL FITNESS OF THE HUMAN SPECIES

Biological fitness means the ability to survive to reproductive age, find mates, and produce offspring. The more offspring an organism produces during its lifetime greater is its biological fitness.

Enhancement of biological fitness occurs at least by two mechanisms: 1) when a species acquires diverse forms of genes and 2) when a species acquires better genes. A species gains diverse types of genes when the females in the species conceive each of its offspring from different males. A species acquires better genes when the females in the species conceive offspring from healthy males.

Capitalism favors monogamy through marriage. This anomaly, as explained before, would make a woman conceive all her children from one man, which results in a lack of genetic diversity in the human species. And also, because of economic reasons, women tend to choose rich men, not necessarily healthy men, as their marriage partners. For these reasons, capitalism does not favor the enhancement of the biological fitness of the human species.

CAPITALISM AND OVERPOPULATION

Overpopulation is a tremendous economic burden both on the family and society alike. The primary cause of the current high rate of population growth is that most women are uneducated and do not have the freedom to decide how many children they would bear. Capitalism favors population overgrowth, mainly of the poor because education is ineffective, people are superstitious or conservative, the poor are mostly uneducated, and women are subordinate to men. It is not surprising that the overpopulation is found only in the developing countries, where the people are both poor and least educated.

PROBLEMS OF THE RICH UNDER CAPITALISM

In capitalism, as one gets richer, one's needs, or rather, perceived needs, also increase accordingly. Then one gets used to these increased needs. Because of this and the higher taxes that the rich pays, the "feeling of wealthy" always evades like a mirage. Moreover, as one's earnings increase, so will their undertakings and the workload, and the resultant physical and mental burdens. In addition to this, the mutual distrust among the people in this system prevents one from sharing the burdens of the increased workload with others and thus burdening one further. That is, as one gets wealthier, more would be the workload, and less would be the ability to enjoy the fruits of one's labor. Moreover, preoccupation in earning can itself prevent people from spending. Besides, even a big industry or business can face losses or become bankrupt at any stage because of the severe competition in this system. No one enjoys competition and not to speak of enjoying the rat race. That is, economic insecurity haunts even the rich. Further, rich people suffer from relative deprivation: feeling discontent by comparing themselves to richer ones. Because of these and also other evils discussed earlier, namely, the class conflict of the poor class with the rich, burdens of family responsibilities, and lack of variety in the entertainment and sexual pleasure, a capitalist system is bad not only for the poor but the rich.

"Some people are so poor, all they have is money."

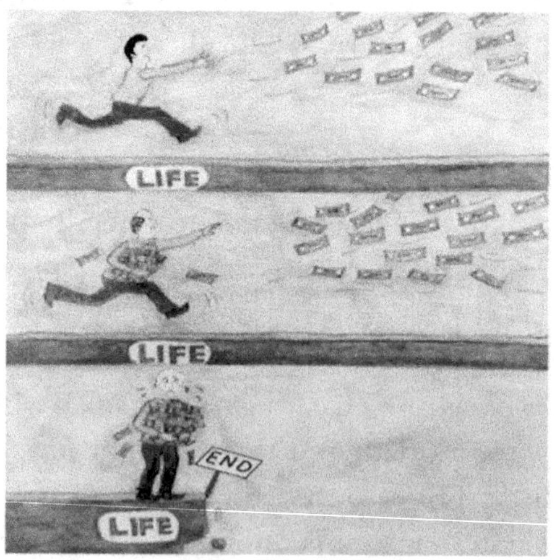

Figure 2: The poor rich man

CAPITALISM AND BEHAVIORAL OR PSYCHOLOGICAL PROBLEMS

Under capitalism, all people are haunted by economic insecurity and burdened by excessive work and family responsibilities. Further, people are often absorbed in the monotonous drudgery of prolonged work hours. They do not get enough leisure nor indulge much in hobbies, sexual pleasure, entertainment, sports, or arts, even if one gets leisure. Therefore, people cannot experience fulfillment, gratification, or contentment in life. As a result, in this system, people not only develop a narrow outlook to life but become easy prey to behavioral problems like personality disorders, paranoia, anxiety, neurosis, depression, drug addiction, and so on.

CAPITALISM AND HUMAN DIVISIVENESS

The hatred, distrust, and divisiveness that exist in society today are a direct result of the nature of societies, past and present. Historical accidents in early communities of humans divided them into many groups. There was an estrangement between the groups that were warring with each other to possess food, territory, and other natural resources. It was here only that the *"ours-theirs"* possessiveness was born. This stage was the first *milestone* in the deviation of the human economy toward the present-day capitalistic economy. Then the economic insecurity of capitalism had its effect on human social behavior, making it more and more divisive. Humans are now a divided lot, though they belong to the same animal species and share common ancestors. A society in which we must compete with others to survive and do not feel secure because other workers threaten our jobs is a breeding ground for hatred, intolerance, paranoia, and divisiveness.

Economic class, gender, race, region, nationality, language, religion, caste, and so on, divide people. Capitalism is thus the main factor that breeds hatred, which prevents people from uniting. This divisiveness, besides, is the cause for all human conflict, violence, and war that are, in turn, the cause for the waste of time, effort, resources, and life and not to speak of the misery and mental stress that conflict, violence, and war bring.

CAPITALISM AND INTERNATIONAL WAR

In addition to unnecessary human suffering and waste of resources, the war also brings famine and epidemics of communicable diseases.

Capitalism causes resource scarcity, greed, and profit motive in people. All these breed crimes—not just gang wars at the local level but even international wars.

Because of the inherent nature of capitalism—profit motive, business expansion, and competition—international wars break out at regular intervals. Wars are being fought over sources of profit: geographical areas of influence and power, foreign markets, resources of fossil fuel and minerals, trade routes, and so on. Also, capitalist society is a breeding ground for hatred and divisiveness because of its economic insecurity. Nations use even race, nationality, religion, and so on, as excuses for war. Another cause for international war in capitalism is the profit motive of the arms manufacturers who lobby and bribe their respective governments to engage in war. Even countries view "encouraging wars" as a great business plan, as it creates profits for many and reduces unemployment. Thus, it may be that war is a racket for some countries, easily the most profitable though the most vicious.

CAN THE WHOLE WORLD BECOME ONE SOCIETY UNDER CAPITALISM?

Given the existing profit motive and human divisiveness, especially nationalism, it is improbable for borders between nations to disappear under capitalism.

CHAPTER 8

A Case for Collective Ownership Based Economy—An Alternative Economic System

IT HAS BEEN RECOGNIZED FOR the last couple of centuries that capitalism is defective—unscientific, inefficient, unjust, and harmful. At present, under capitalism, it is not "economically feasible" to solve many of the problems that humans face because such measures bring down profits. There has been consensus among many that abolishing capitalism altogether will mean the removal of the source of the cause of much of human suffering, and that a radical change in our economic system that eliminates economic insecurity would bring more prosperity, peace, and happiness to humans than can be done by any other social change that one can ever think of.

For a couple of centuries, many have conceived *socialist economic models* as a better alternative to capitalism. This socialist movement believes that capitalism cannot meet the needs of the majority of the people in the world, and capitalism must be replaced by a socialist economy to meet the needs of all.

Though there is much agreement on the meaning of "capitalism," people still differ much on the meaning and description of the "socialist model of economy."

WHY CALL IT COLLECTIVE OWNERSHIP BASED ECONOMY

The economic model proposed here can be called socialism, communism, collectivism, collective economy, resource-based economy, or whatever. However, "what it is" is the issue and not "what it is called." The economic model proposed in this book resembles the existing models of socialist economic systems a lot. The model is called "*Collective Ownership Based Economy*" (COBE) because *collective ownership* is the most fundamental and central tenet of a truly socialist economic model.

Tenets of the Proposed Collective Ownership Based Economy (COBE)

CAPITALISM IS THE ECONOMIC SYSTEM that has been there the world over for a long time, and COBE, as proposed here, has not been in practice so far anywhere in the world.

The economic model proposed here, aims mainly at eliminating the drawbacks of capitalism so that all people would be free of economic insecurity and enjoy prosperity, peace, and happiness.

Thus, the principles of the proposed economic system are constructed primarily with the objective of forming a better social arrangement for attaining abundance instead of scarcity, unlike capitalism, of goods and services for all, along with maintaining healthy local, regional, and global ecosystems.

The *five* tenets of the proposed Collective Ownership Based Economy (COBE) are as follows:

* *Collective ownership* of the wealth of the society by all its members
* *Collective work* in the production and distribution of goods and services by all members according to their abilities

* ***Free access** to goods and services* to all members according to their needs and doing away with trade and the monetary system
* *Voluntary work/labor*
* *Decision making by democracy*

COLLECTIVE OWNERSHIP

Only *equality* makes all members of a society prosperous, peaceful, and happy, and only *economic equality* is true *equality*. All people have an equal stake in, and so equal right on, the wealth of the society. Economic equality means all members of society possess an equal amount of wealth or resources. There is only one way to make it absolutely and exactly equal—*collective ownership* of the wealth of the society by all its members. Thus it involves doing away with the capitalist system of *private ownership of wealth*. That is, there will not be an owner class. Note, however, that an individual can still possess *personal belongings* such as toothbrush and undergarments. Thus, the central tenet of the proposed model of economy is *collective ownership* or *common ownership* or *common heritage*. Collective ownership, the first and the most fundamental tenet, implies all the other *four* tenets of the proposed economy, as explained below.

If the society needs to be changed to one of collective ownership of resources, why would the rich accept it? Why would they give up their possessed wealth? Is the idea practicable? This question will be addressed later after completing the full description of COBE.

COLLECTIVE WORK

If its members collectively own the resources of a society, it implies that *collective work or endeavour* by all people would run the community wherein all will have equal responsibility, right, and opportunity to be involved in working for the society according to individual ability.

FREE ACCESS TO GOODS AND SERVICES TO ALL MEMBERS ACCORDING TO THEIR NEEDS AND DOING AWAY WITH TRADE AND THE MONETARY SYSTEM

Collective ownership also implies that there will not be "buying and selling" or trade of goods and services, which is a necessity only under capitalism because of its system of *private ownership of wealth*. Production, under COBE, will be for the use and not for sale. Thus, all the members of the society will have *free access to all their needs* or goods and services according to their needs. That is, the needs of people will be met *free of cost*. Therefore, there will also not be the *monetary system*; that is, *money* as a medium of exchange will not be there, unlike the case of the capitalist system.

VOLUNTARY WORK/LABOR

No *buying and selling* and *free access to all needs* also imply that work, *labor, or employment* will have to be *voluntary*—that is, without any compulsion to work. The employment will be according to one's ability.

Humans are born lazy. Therefore, they work only if there is an incentive as in capitalism. So, COBE, which is based on the free provision of people's needs and voluntary employment, cannot succeed. Why would people work if they don't have to? This question too, will be addressed later after completing the full description of COBE.

DECISION MAKING BY DEMOCRACY

If collective ownership and collective endeavor are the basis for the economic system, it also implies that everyone has a stake in how the society is organized and run. Therefore, everybody will have an equal right to participate in the social decisions that affect them. Thus the *decision-making body* of the society will have to be constituted *democratically*. This body will democratically decide how society is to be organized and run.

CHAPTER 10

Present Status of Socialist Economies

Note that the proposed system in this book has never been tried anywhere in the world before.

Socialism, in its rudimentary form, was conceived a couple of centuries ago. It has been implemented and has been successful too, to varying extents. Still, the success that socialist economies got so far is much less than they deserve.

A prominent reason for the failure of socialist economies thus far is that it has only been partial socialism when seen in the light of features of COBE proposed above. The shortcoming of such "socialism" is that it has still retained some capitalist principles—mainly, the system of private property and, hence, also the usage of money. Since private property and money have been an integral part of human life for a long time in history, it must have been hard for economic thinkers to imagine a society without their use.

Another important reason for the failure of socialist economies is that implementation of the economy has been through dictatorship instead of democracy. Mention must be made, in this regard, of Karl Marx (1818–1883), a brilliant social scientist of his times. His contribution to the socialist economy is that he made an accurate scientific analysis of the faulty, and so, the harmful nature of capitalism. However, his suggestion of an alternative system, *communism*, is defective. Democracy was not his strong point. He advocated "dictatorship of the proletariat or workers". He also believed that capitalism would collapse on its own. The dictators of the former Soviet Union, China, and so on, exploited the ideas of Karl Marx to snatch political power only to oppress people for personal gains. The derogatory meaning that the terms 'socialism' and 'communism' have acquired is because of such exploitations.

The socialism of "communist" nations of past and present has been administered through military or State dictatorship, which is hence dictatorship-socialism or autocratic-socialism. Even though the evils of a dictatorship-socialism are due to dictatorship, even socialism has been wrongly thought to be ineffective and harmful because of its association with dictatorship. The lesson to be learned is that a system cannot be imposed on people regardless of its merits. A popular revolt against a dictatorship regime is inevitable. Instead, the merits have to be explained to people, and their confidence and consent have to be obtained before implementing it. That is, if the socialist economy as an economic system has merit, it has to stand the test of democracy before being implemented.

Because of these unsuccessful implementations, socialist economy is almost globally misunderstood and misrepresented, and presently associated with low popularity and stigma. So low is the popularity of socialism that even the present-day mainstream economists are busy debating how one capitalist policy is better or worse than another capitalist policy. But they rarely take up the crucial and more fundamental debate of *capitalism* versus the *socialist economy*.

CHAPTER 11

Organizations Actively Involved in Socialist or Socialist-Like Movements at Present

Notable organizations actively involved in socialist or socialist-like movements at present are World Socialist Movement (WSM), Resource Based Economy (RBE) of The Venus Project, Natural Law Resource Based Economy (NLRBE) of The Zeitgeist Movement, and The Money Free Party (an international political party). They have made advances in conceptualizing socialist or socialist-like systems that are somewhat similar to the proposed socialist system in this book.

WSM is an organization that began with the founding of the Socialist Party of Great Britain in 1904. The Companion Parties of Socialism, which make up the WSM, are those parties sharing an understanding of what socialism means, how to establish socialism, and scientific analysis of past and current society.

It stands for the sole aim of establishing a global system of society in which there will be common ownership and democratic control of the world's natural and industrial resources. That is, WSM has conceptualized a socialist system that advocates both *collective ownership* and *democracy*.

Both RBE and NLRBE advocate *collective ownership* and have done an in-depth scientific analysis of faults of the current economic system—capitalism or market economy. They have developed well-researched and advanced technological and industrial concepts of society building. They do not believe much in democracy though. They rely more on advanced technology like the computer and artificial intelligence (AI) to take over the job of decision making. However, the following question arises: Would rely on technology for decision-making turns into a dictatorship by the technologists or technocracy?

Both WSM and RBE believe that just one or a few countries cannot establish the new economic order in isolation, and must be done globally when all the countries accept it.

RBE, somewhat like Karl Marx, believes that capitalism will eventually collapse on its own.

The Money Free Party is an international political party that is active in sixteen countries. The party advocates for a resource-based economy (RBE).

CHAPTER 12

How Replacing Capitalism with the Proposed COBE Will Help Overcome the Ills of the Society and Bring Prosperity, Peace, and Happiness for All

(NOTE: SOME OF THE EXPLANATIONS in this section are long, and a few are repetitive. That is because the proposed COBE will be a fundamental structural change to society. Collective ownership of resources, free access to the needs of the people, voluntary work/ labor, and a society without currency—all of these are unknown, unheard of, and difficult to imagine as practicable for most people. For the vast majority of people, the current society and its system appear to be normal. Everyone around them seems to be working and behaving in almost the same way, creating in their minds an impression of normality. People tend to accept as true and normal the things they repeatedly see, hear, and read, day in and day out. That is further compounded by the fact that people have a vast range of divisive opinions and polarization—nationalistic, political, racial, religious, and so on. Also, the socialist economy is almost globally misunderstood and misrepresented and is presently associated with low popularity and stigma.)

The advantages to society if the proposed COBE is adopted as an economic system in place of capitalism will be, in simple words, mainly due to the absence of the adverse effects of the capitalist system.

COBE Will Exist as One Big Single Economic Unit — The Most Efficient Economic System

In COBE, the whole society (or nation or the world) will exist as one big single economic unit, unlike capitalism, in which the entire society exists as small multiple (millions of) independent economic units. Therefore, the benefits (cost-effectiveness) of large-scale operation (economies of scale) would be maximal in COBE. That is, in this system, both material abundance and leisure for human beings would be maximal. This benefit due to economies of scale is the main advantage of COBE, and the benefit is enormous.

When global society is a possibility, the scale of operation will be larger, and the benefits will be huger.

For this reason, COBE is scientific and, hence, the most efficient economic system. *Material abundance*, as against *scarcity*, unlike capitalism, is thus the hallmark of COBE.

Material abundance is the main advantage of COBE as an economic system.

Control, Planning, and Coordination of the Economy in COBE

Since, in COBE, the economy of society will exist as a single unit, operational efficiency would be maximal. It would be easier to have control between various economic subunits. Economic planning would also be more straightforward, and there will not be a wasteful overproduction of some goods or underproduction of some other. That is, shortages, overruns, and wastages could be eliminated. So, that way also, COBE as an economic system is more efficient than capitalism.

Further, since COBE will be a single unit, unlike the capitalist system, it would allow the adoption of a cybernated system for coordination of the economy of the society. Cybernated system is useful in maintaining a steady-state dynamic balance between production, distribution, and society's needs. In a society with cybernated technology, human labor in production, distribution of goods and services, and even administration can be reduced drastically.

(Cybernetics is the science of applying control and communication in a machine, industry, or even an organization like human society. Most of the technology needed for such management is currently available. Cybernetics involving programs with electronic sensor systems, resource-tracking technology, industrial electronic feedback technology, and communications networks have been developing for industries. Hewlett-Packard Company has developed what it calls "A Central Nervous System for the Earth" [2009])

COBE AND PROFIT MOTIVE

There will be no profit motive in COBE. Unlike capitalism, the production of commodities would be according to the needs of the society, and not according to the extent of the profit motive of the producers. Thus, unlike capitalism, there will be no wastes due to overproduction of goods-services; no low quality goods-services (goods will be built to be durable); no wastes on the advertisement and the accompanying excess labor; no artificially created scarcity; no wastes of goods due to use-and-throw culture (goods will be repaired and recycled); no development among people of the unhealthy culture of consumerism.

No Unemployment, Underemployment, and Misemployment in COBE

There is no question of unemployment in COBE as people will work voluntarily and will have free access to their needs.

COBE and Social Behavior

In COBE, unlike capitalism, there will be material abundance; therefore, there will not be economic insecurity. Also, meeting of an individual's needs will depend on the collective productivity of society, not on individual productivity. That is, in a COBE society, satisfying an individual's needs will be the result of meeting everyone's needs. Put another way, the only way that an individual can enhance the satisfaction of one's own needs will be by working for the enhancement of the fulfillment of the whole society's needs. It is enlightened and extended self-interest that will work for all the members of the society. Further, in COBE, all people's needs will be met free of cost depending on the individual need.

Therefore, there will be *cooperation* and *mutual trust* in the affairs of people instead of counterproductive behavior—*possessiveness, rivalry, greed, jealousy, mutual distrust,* and so on, which are just products of capitalism, as discussed before under "Capitalism, Economic Insecurity, and Social Behavior." The economic conditions of COBE are conducive to the innate human behavior, which is *being social*—mutually cooperative and compassionate. That is, COBE would facilitate the development of a warm, friendly, and supportive ambiance.

The fact that even under capitalism we see, many times, people obtain satisfaction from helping others is proof that humans are innately and potentially compassionate. Few enjoy participating in the rat race.

Besides, since there will not be possession of wealth in COBE, there will not be the distortion of value system, priorities, preferences, and attitudes in people; also, people would not become economic-status conscious nor egoistic.

Cooperation brings out the "best" in us.
Competition brings out the "beast" in us.

It is now highly feasible to take care of everybody on
earth at a "higher standard of living than any have ever
known." It no longer has to be you or me. Selfishness
is unnecessary and henceforth unrationalizable
as mandated by survival. War is obsolete.

—R. BUCKMINSTER FULLER, 1895–1983, ARCHITECT, SYSTEMS
THEORIST, AUTHOR, DESIGNER, AND INVENTOR

COBE AND DEMOCRACY

In COBE, since personal earnings or wealth will not exist, people enter the field of legislation or politics out of their interest and not for accumulating wealth. Besides, in this system, since the society or administration or government will bear the costs of election (state funding of elections), no legislative or political talent of any people will go untapped, unlike the case of capitalism, where the poor cannot afford to contest the elections. Because of these, there will be a real democracy; therefore, the administration or government will be efficient, and the progress of society and civilization will not be hindered, unlike capitalism.

No Economic Inequality and Class Struggle in COBE

COBE will be a system of common ownership, where there will be neither private wealth nor competition to acquire it. Meeting of people's needs will depend not on one's earnings, unlike capitalism, but on the productivity of the society, and the needs of all people will be met free depending on the individual need. Since there will not be the poor-rich economic classes, there will be no basis for interclass antagonism nor its costly adverse effects—theft, robbery, riots, armed insurgency, terrorism, and war.

No Periodic Recession in COBE

Since there will not be profit motive (production of commodities would be according to the needs of the society), there is no question of the danger of periodic recession in COBE.

In COBE There Will Be No Currency, Bank, Tax system, Insurance, Advertisement, Police, Judiciary, and Military

In COBE, as the needs of people will be met free of cost, there will not be the need for the medium of exchange, and therefore, there will also not be wastage of materials and labor in the form of currency, banks, insurance, and so on.

Besides, since there will not be any economic insecurity in people or nations, there will not be any crime or war (when all countries embrace COBE). Hence police, judiciary, and military will become redundant, saving, again, material and labor on the one hand and eliminating human suffering on the other. Police, prisons, and judiciary would no longer be necessary when there is free access to all goods and services. However, during the initial period after the transition to COBE, social workers and behavior therapists might be required to work with police and judiciary. Later all their services could be progressively reduced in response to the observed reduction of crimes.

COBE AND ECOLOGICAL BALANCE

In a COBE world, there will be no profit or greed to acquire wealth indiscriminately. Production will be for satisfying human needs and not for accumulating wealth. There will be cooperation instead of competition. Planning, control, and coordination of the economy will be easier than in capitalism, as in COBE the economy of society will exist as a single unit. Therefore, reclaiming and restoring a healthy ecosystem will be much easier and that would be considered a normal part of all decision making in a COBE.

COBE AND UTILIZATION OF AVAILABLE NEWER SCIENTIFIC TECHNOLOGIES

In COBE, there will not be any constraints, unlike capitalism, to utilize available newer knowledge and technologies, as a COBE is not based on profit-making, and there is no question of loss of business or job. So a COBE society will use science and technology sustainably to their fullest potential to supply every human being with all the material goods for a comfortable and enjoyable life.

No Commercialization of Education, Healthcare, Entertainment, and Art in COBE

In COBE, there is no profit motive; dangers of commercialization of education, healthcare, entertainment, and art will not be there. So their qualities will not get compromised.

Workplace Satisfaction under COBE

Under the proposed COBE, labor is voluntary, and so, the problem of dissatisfaction at the workplace doesn't arise.

COBE and Leisure

Under the proposed COBE, the whole of society will be a single economic unit. So it takes full advantage of economies of scale (large-scale operation). One of the benefits of this is that there will be an enormous reduction in labor and workforce requirements. Under COBE, many jobs (dealing with banking, tax system, insurance, advertisement, police, judiciary, and military) will become redundant or irrelevant and will not be required at all. Moreover, a COBE society will use science and technology that we already know sustainably to their fullest potential to provide all people a high standard of living. Mechanization, massive construction machines, automation, robotics, information technology, artificial intelligence, cybernetics, 3-D printing technology, self-driven vehicles, and so on can almost eliminate the need for human labor. Also, machines can completely replace humans for doing all strenuous, unpleasant, and monotonous work. Besides, innovations in science and technology can easily provide more abundance and, hence, more leisure to every individual in society.

Thus, COBE, being a system that is consistent with modern developments in technology, would grant individuals the opportunity to pursue their true individuality and creativity through the progressive reduction of necessary work time.

"Everyone can enjoy a life of luxurious leisure if the machine-produced wealth is shared, or most people can end up miserably poor if the machine-owners successfully lobby against wealth redistribution."—Stephen Hawking

No Educational Burden and Its Effect on Children's and Students' Creativity in COBE

The more intelligent and educated the children are, the better for all others, and the more robust would be the future society. It is the environment that molds people, and so, a healthy learning environment needs to be created. There will not be the unemployment problem in COBE, unlike capitalism. Therefore, there will be no competition among people for jobs. Hence the education system will not overburden the students with unnecessary information and, at the same time, examinations also will not be competitive. That will be a huge relief for students. So the pursuance of their individuality and also the budding of their creativity will not be suppressed.

Education in a COBE will give more emphasis on basic science, history, geography, biology (including evolution, human biology, and behavior science), and communication skills in a way that will make children responsible and caring citizens. More emphasis will also be given to problem-based learning, hands-on experience, and learning from interacting directly with the physical surroundings. People will be educated not only about the proposed COBE system but the importance of a healthy ecosystem. The transition from the current model to the COBE one, in any case, will automatically transform the education system in such ways as mentioned above because most of the educational ills of the present society are the direct consequence of the faults and restraints of capitalism.

SUPERSTITIONS UNDER COBE

In COBE, there will not be private wealth, the rich and poor classes, unemployment, and the government's negligence of education. So, unlike capitalism, there will not be the question of exploitation and fraud. Thus, conditions will not be favorable for the growth of superstitions. That is, if a society were to change from capitalism to COBE, superstitions would die a natural death.

BURDENS ON THE HEAD OF THE FAMILY UNDER COBE

Under COBE, since the provision of all individuals' needs will be the responsibility of the society or the government, family responsibilities will burden no one. Thus in a COBE system, the community will take over the economic responsibilities of the *father,* the *husband,* or the head of the family.

COBE AND LAZINESS

In COBE, the education system will not overburden children with excess and unnecessary information; there will be free access to the needs of the people; employment will be voluntary; people can go after the works they are interested in; people will have lots of leisure. Therefore, this system, unlike capitalism, will not suppress the born-dynamic nature of human beings. So there will be no reason for the manifestation of laziness in people.

COBE AND ECONOMIC EMANCIPATION OF WOMEN

Under COBE, no woman (nor man) will have the problem of unemployment and lack of education; free provision of needs and childcare will be the responsibilities of the society, which will take over the economic roles of the *father, husband,* or the head of the family; superstition and conservatism would take a backstage. All these will ensure the economic emancipation of women. That is, women would not be economically dependent upon men, unlike capitalism, where the majority of women are.

SEXUAL PRACTICE UNDER COBE

In COBE, there will be free access to all needs, including health and education for all, and society will take over the responsibilities of the *husband* in taking care of women, especially during pregnancy and childcare. Therefore, there will not be any social pressure on people to enter the marriage contract for the sake of sex. Thus the taboo of sex outside marriage will disappear and so will the restriction on sexual freedom. People would live their sexual lives the way they want, without society telling them how to.

In turn, sexual freedom will go a long way in mitigating all the adverse effects of sexual deprivation, namely, obsession with sex, sexual perversions, rape, prostitution, sexually transmitted diseases, marital disharmony, divorce, lack of motivation, and drug addiction.

Can the sexual relationship between people be predicted in a COBE Society?

In all probability, more and more people would opt for a *polyamorous relationship* under COBE. (Polyamorous relationship means having multiple sexually and/or romantically committed relationships at the same time, with the knowledge of all partners involved.)

Will the people go for nudism?

Yes, it looks like it will be so whenever the climate permits to be so. Capitalism is the reason for monogamous marriage; the result, in turn, is that sex outside marriage has become a taboo. So, clothing one's body, which shields the *prying eyes*, is the consequence of this taboo. Male dominance could be another reason for the prevailing clothing practice.

FREEDOM FOR WOMEN TO DECIDE ABOUT CHILD CONCEPTION UNDER COBE

In COBE, women will have the freedom to choose how many children to conceive and from whom to conceive each of them because of their economic and sexual emancipation, freedom from the compulsion of marriage, and absence of male domination.

COBE AND ENHANCEMENT OF BIOLOGICAL FITNESS

Under COBE, a child will need only a mother and not a father as the role of the father will be taken over by the society; there will be sexual emancipation (even of women); people will be educated in contraception as the education system will be efficient. COBE, therefore, will allow women to mate with any men they wish to but conceive only from men of their choice. Naturally, women will 1) tend to conceive not more than one child from a single man because they tend to go for variety while seeking sexual pleasure, and 2) tend to conceive from *healthy and sexually attractive men*, which amounts to same as *men with healthy genetic heritage*. This tendency serves as a natural mechanism for the enhancement of biological fitness (genetic improvement) of the species over time. This fact would be one more biological proof to say that COBE is complementary or favorable to innate human nature.

RATE OF POPULATION GROWTH UNDER COBE

As noted earlier, the overpopulation problem is found only in the developing countries, where the people are both poor and least educated. This problem will not be there in a COBE society. Because in this system, there will be no rich and poor classes, education will be effective, and superstitions and conservatism will disappear on its own. And most importantly, women will be economically emancipated and will have the freedom to decide the number of children that they would conceive.

COBE AND THE PROBLEMS OF THE RICH

In COBE, there will be no poor and wealthy classes; all the work of the society will be under the government's control, the needs of all will be met free of cost, no one will be haunted by economic insecurity, and there will be lots of leisure. The work, therefore, will not burden the physical and mental health. Besides, there will be no family responsibilities in this system. Because of these reasons, though the rich are better off than poor in capitalism, any citizen of a COBE society will be better off than any citizen, including the rich, of a capitalist society.

BEHAVIORAL OR PSYCHOLOGICAL PROBLEMS UNDER COBE

Under COBE, there will not be economic insecurity, and nobody will be burdened with excessive work nor family responsibilities. People can indulge in entertainment, sports, and arts as there will be lots of leisure. Also, there will be neither the lack of sensual pleasures nor the lack of variety in them. Therefore, people will have the opportunity to pursue the development of their real individuality and creativity and experience contentment in life. The measure of success, in COBE, would be the extent of leading a self-fulfilling life—the fulfillment of one's interests and pursuits rather than the extent of acquiring wealth and power. Therefore, in this system, unlike capitalism, people not only will develop a broad outlook on life but would not be prey to behavioral problems like paranoia, anxiety, neurosis, depression, drug addiction, and so on.

COBE and Human Unity

Under COBE, all the wealth of society will be the common heritage of all its people (collective ownership). The only way that an individual can enhance the satisfaction of one's own needs will be by working in a way that increases the fulfillment of the needs of society as a whole. It is enlightened and extended self-interest that would work for all people of the society. Therefore, people will cooperate in their work for the betterment of the whole society. So there will not be any conflict in the interests of people, unlike the case of capitalism. These conditions of COBE will create an environment where people will recognize that all of them are descendants of the same ancestors and members of the same species. In all probability, this will make all people of the world feel like they are part of one big worldwide family.

Thus, COBE will favor human unity by breaking the barriers like economic class, gender, nationality, region, language, race, religion, caste, creed, and so on. In other words, COBE will remove all human conflict, violence, and war, which in turn eliminates wastes of time, effort, resources, life, and the misery and mental stress that conflict, violence, and war bring.

COBE and War

Under COBE, the causes for human divisiveness will not exist, and neither the profit motive, which are the causes of war. However, to entirely do away with war, COBE needs to be adopted all over the world.

THE WHOLE WORLD AS ONE SOCIETY — MORE BENEFIT DUE TO COBE

A COBE nation would not exhibit, as explained before, aggressiveness and imperialism against other countries. Also, other nations would get convinced of the economic efficiency of the COBE countries and so would be bound to follow COBE. Besides, since larger the size of an economic unit more is the benefits (economies of scale), there is much possibility of disappearance of borders between nations, leading to their merger. One more factor in COBE that favors the formation of a single world society is that it would eliminate the interhuman conflict and the divisiveness of capitalism. That is, the possibility of a union of all nations in the world as a single economic unit forming a single world society, and therefore, of further increase of prosperity, happiness, and peace for the human species, is there only under COBE.

CHAPTER 13

Conclusion in Short

IN SHORT, THE CAUSE FOR almost all preventable human sufferings is the "germ" called capitalism. The proposed COBE is the panacea for these ills. Also, from another perspective, it is difficult to imagine the incredible level of prosperity, peace, and happiness a society might achieve once inefficient and oppressive factors of capitalism are removed.

CHAPTER 14

Answers for Some Possible "Objections" to COBE

> *If the society needs to be changed to one of collective ownership of resources, why would the rich accept it? Why would they give up their possessed wealth? Is the idea practicable?*

THE ANSWER TO THIS OBJECTION is this: 1) The rich are a small minority, so, in a democracy, they will have minimal decision-making power. 2) Under the proposed COBE, even the rich will benefit, as explained in a previous section. Though the rich are relatively better off than the poor under the current economic system, they will be better off under the proposed COBE than they are under the current system. 3) Being rich does not mean that they are evil. Even they are human and, so, compassionate. The rich, therefore, if convinced of the benefits of the proposed COBE, would be happy about the change that COBE would bring—the prospect of the end of wars, crimes, poverty, debt, and other hardships that humans are facing at present and also the knowledge that everyone will be having a high standard of life.

> *Humans are born lazy. Therefore, they do not work if there isn't any incentive. So, COBE, which is based on the free provision of*

people's needs and voluntary employment, cannot succeed. Why would people work if they don't have to?

People enjoy activities that are interesting and that create useful things. It is the nature of the work that makes it enjoyable.

You don't have to work a single day in your life if you get paid for doing what you enjoy.

Humans are born dynamic, helpful, and compassionate.

If we find many people lazy, selfish, and lacking in compassion, that is because of the conditioning by the capitalist economic system, as explained before. We tend to superimpose current capitalist adverse effects on the new COBE model, erroneously.

It is the drudgery, monotonous nature of work, underemployment (low-paying jobs), and misemployment that make people lazy under capitalism. People tend to accept as normal the things they see and hear over and over again. We have been observing laziness in people and, so, are conditioned to believe that humans are lazy by nature (born lazy), not knowing that laziness is just a product of the faulty capitalist economic system.

The desire for exceptional wealth is by no means a necessary stimulus to work. We have been conditioned to believe that monetary rewards motivate people. A vast majority of people work not to get rich but to meet the basic needs, and the rags-to-riches stories are more in fiction than in reality. Is the statement "America is a place of unparalleled opportunity", a fact or mere rhetoric? Studies show that the upward economic mobility of lower-rung people in the United States is a myth (*Science Daily*, 2012; *New York Times*, 2012). In the current economic model, most of the people are in pursuit of money for survival. The monetary incentive has corrupted the innate natural incentive system in humans—the pleasure one gets out of exploring, learning, and creating.

In the new economic model, each member's labor will contribute to the prosperity of society. More the prosperity of the society as a whole more would be the satisfaction of each member's needs. If members of a COBE society know the above facts, the merits of COBE, and the demerits of capitalism, as discussed before, the above objection does not apply to COBE.

Moreover, COBE, as explained before, will create an abundance of wealth and lots of leisure as well because it allows taking full benefits of large-scale operation, and science and technology (such as automation, robotics, and artificial intelligence). Further, under COBE, most of the jobs will become redundant and, so, will not be required. In other words, COBE will reduce the need for human labor to a large extent. Besides, machines can completely replace humans for doing all dangerous, strenuous, unpleasant, and monotonous works.

Furthermore, it is a basic nature of humans to work voluntarily. Even in competition-oriented capitalism, we see people donate services, materials, and money to those who are affected by natural disasters, diseases, and so on. The incentive for such acts is the compassion and the sense of contribution. However, the overall motivation is still money in the present society.

Besides, in a society where one gets free access to all needs, people will be grateful to the community. They will volunteer to work willingly without feeling *lazy*. Since the proposed COBE system will serve everyone, human values will change, and many would likely be motivated to take up more hours of labor.

Moreover, when people will be convinced about the benefits of the proposed COBE, one more incentive, which will propel people to work, will be the prospect of the end of wars, crimes, poverty, debt, and other hardships that humans are facing at present and also the knowledge that everyone will be having a high standard of life.

One can predict that under COBE, there would be an unemployment problem of another kind—people will want to volunteer to be employed. But, the COBE society will not be able to engage all because only a small number of personnel is required to run the proposed model of COBE society.

What would you do if you lived in a community where you had free access to everything you needed and didn't have to work for a living—would you work voluntarily in that community, even if you don't have to?

* *One gathers from what one has observed till now that government or public undertakings usually run under loss. Therefore, COBE, which is essentially a public undertaking, will not be successful.*

However, the inefficiency of the present governments, as explained before, is because of the defects of capitalism. The current governments, even though democratic, act mostly in the interests of capitalists. Besides, far from being inefficient, how a COBE system, as proposed in this book, will be much efficient is also explained before. Therefore, this objection does not hold good for a COBE administration.

* *Humans are basically selfish and greedy in nature. Therefore, COBE, which runs on cooperation, cannot succeed.*

Humans are the most social among all social animals. Being a social animal is evolutionarily determined. Therefore, humans are genetically designed to be social. So the basic nature of humans is *being-social*. Innate behaviors that also come along with being a social animal are being cooperative with and helpful and compassionate to fellow humans. Thus humans are not born selfish or greedy. The selfishness and greediness that we see in humans at present are, as explained before, because of the conditions of the capitalist economic system. Capitalism as an economic system is based on private wealth accumulation, which encourages the development of mutual competition, selfishness, greed, rivalry, mutual distrust, and so on in humans, as discussed before. It is more like "one benefits at the cost of others." In COBE, which is based on collective ownership of society's wealth, there will be cooperation, and humans will not have the antisocial behaviors that we see under capitalism. In a COBE society, satisfying an individual's needs is the result of meeting everyone's needs. Self-interest becomes social interest. It is like "one benefits because all benefit."

* **COBE** *is beneficial only for ordinary people and not for the talented.*

However, the truth is that **COBE** will be beneficial for the talented as well as the ordinary. In contrast, capitalism is beneficial only for the born-rich and the gifted, and not for the ordinary. Nobody's talent will be suppressed in COBE since education will be effective, and also there is neither money nor its influences, unlike in capitalism. Besides, in COBE, since there will be more freedom to choose employment of one's interest, unlike in capitalism, any talented person can seek employment of their interest. Also, any COBE citizen, as explained before, will enjoy more prosperity, peace, and happiness than a capitalist citizen of any talent. A talented person in COBE will not be discontent; on the contrary, they will always feel indebted to the COBE society.

> *Survival of the fittest is the law of evolution of life. Therefore, capitalism, which involves competition, is better than COBE, which requires cooperation.*

Survival of the fittest does not mean that there would be competition or war between individuals, as in capitalism, where some would be deprived of prosperity, peace, and happiness while some others would be physically eliminated. It only means that the copies of the fittest individuals or genes of a species get more representations in the future generations of that species. How COBE favors, instead of opposing, natural genetic improvement is already explained.

> *Economic freedom (freedom in choosing employment and consumer items) is more in capitalism than in COBE.*

True freedom is being able to live life without feeling economic insecurity. Today, true freedom is enjoyed to some extent only by the wealthy. How work opportunities will be more in COBE, and the inevitable unemployment and underemployment in capitalism is already dealt with. Moreover, consumer choice is more in appearances than in quality because of the profit motive in capitalism. This so-called variety is forced to the consumer through advertisement. Only COBE can provide real variety in consumer items.

> *COBE is suitable only for the developing nations and not for the developed ones.*

However, the developed nations are developed mainly because of their low population, abundant natural resources, and well-developed democratic system, and not because of capitalism. If they change from the inefficient capitalist economy to efficient COBE, they will enjoy a further increase in their prosperity.

> *In COBE, sexual freedom will lead to an increase in the incidence of sexually transmitted diseases, including the dreaded AIDS.*

The causes for sexually transmitted diseases are prostitution, ignorance of the people about these diseases, and negligence by the governmental healthcare systems. However, since these causes can exist, as explained before, only in a capitalist system but not in a COBE, these diseases will not exist in the latter.

> *COBE is antireligious*

COBE is neither antireligion nor the one that uses force to suppress religion. All superstitions exist under capitalism for exploiting the gullible for money and power. In COBE, there will not be private property, money, or profit-making. Therefore, superstitions will disappear on their own; that is, people stop practicing superstitions on their own. Thus, there is no question of opposing religion or forcing people to quit religion.

> *The erstwhile Soviet Union, which pioneered the adoption of the socialist system, has itself given it up. Therefore, COBE is not worth adopting.*

The erstwhile Soviet Union, which claimed to be socialist, was, in reality, dictatorship capitalists or State capitalists with a semblance of socialism. The former Soviet Union still had private property, money, and buying and selling. The primary cause for the political changes in the former Soviet Union (and some East European nations) was the rebellious upsurges of the people against the dictatorship of the government and not because of the socialist system.

* *Mixed economy, which is a combination of the merits of both capitalism and COBE, is better than either pure capitalism or pure COBE.*

Capitalism, as explained before, does not have even single merit but only demerits. So it follows that pure capitalism is worse than the mixed economy and pure *COBE* is the best. It's like, for drinking purposes, pure mud is worse than muddy water, and clean water is the best.

CHAPTER 15

Action Plan to Establish COBE

THE MORE THE NUMBER OF countries adopts the proposed COBE system, the better for all people in the world. *So the ultimate goal is to establish COBE all over the world.*

COBE cannot be forced on people, despite its merits. A dictatorial/authoritarian government would not only be inefficient but be power abusive since there is no popular control. Therefore, a popular revolt against such a government is inevitable.

Transition to COBE, therefore, needs to be brought about only through peaceful and democratic processes, including activism and awareness campaigns, both short- and long term.

The measures to be taken up for the transition could be both *direct* and *indirect*.

The direct measure is to create awareness and understanding, and mobilize support for the proposed model of COBE among the majority of people—that is, convincing the people of the meaning and benefits of COBE or the need of a fundamental reconstruction of the society into a COBE system. It boils down, ultimately, to convincing people that 'economic equality' or 'collective ownership' is their 'human right' so that they demand it. Only the majority acting consciously in its interests can create COBE by itself. While campaigning for the system change, one needs to appeal to people's reason, cooperativeness, and compassion. Note that all are potentially reasonable, cooperative, and compassionate.

That said, convincing the people about the benefits of the proposed COBE might seem daunting because, as noted earlier, the proposed economic system will be a fundamental structural change to society. Collective ownership of resources, free access to the needs of the people, voluntary work/labor, society without currency—all of these are unknown, unheard of, and difficult to imagine as practicable for most people. For the vast majority of people, the current society and its system appear to be normal. Everyone around them seems to be working and behaving in almost the same manner, creating perceived normality. People tend to accept as true and normal the things they repeatedly see, hear, and read, day in and day out. That is further compounded by the fact that people have a vast range of divisive opinions and polarization (nationalistic, political, racial, religious, and so on).

Convincing the people of the meaning and benefits of the proposed COBE needs to be systematically and logistically carried out, with a multipronged approach. Consider the challenge of convincing the uneducated/illiterate who constitute a majority, especially in the developing countries. They need to be educated with at least some basic knowledge, just enough for them to understand the proposed social system change.

The first and foremost, direct and the mainstay measure required to establish COBE system is giving wide publicity to the proposed COBE using all types of media to create consensus worldwide. Publicity could be done just how it needs to be done when any new idea requires to be spread among people. Expose the public to new possibilities of social order for the benefit of all—through word of mouth, mass online petitions, publications, videos, websites, TV shows, movies, and so on.

Meanwhile, until that time when the society is ready for establishing COBE, other measures that indirectly hasten the transition to COBE could be taken up simultaneously.

These indirect measures, which need to be embarked globally, could be *mobilizing support to the following:*

1) Mobilize support to all organized protests for an end to inequality, poverty, scarcity, homelessness, crime, political corruption, war, environmental destruction, and so on. Some recent examples of such movements, for which support need to be mobilized, are "green" economy by environmentalists, "Occupy Wall Street" (2011) by civil rights groups, and "Pro-Gun Control March for Our Lives" students' rallies across the United States and other countries (March 2018). Iceland is the best example of a country where the Prime Minister had to step down in April 2016 mainly because of the growing people's protests over "Panama Papers Scandal".

2) Mobilize support to all existing socialist political parties and socialist forces and movements

3) Mobilize support to all *welfare state* policies, including *universal basic income*

4) Mobilize support to all democratic forces and movements in all dictatorship/authoritarian countries to change over to the democratic system

5) Mobilize support to all democratic reforms and reform movements

CHAPTER 16

Giving Publicity to COBE— Role of Democracy

THE IMPORTANCE OF DEMOCRACY IN bringing about the transformation of the existing capitalist system to COBE cannot be overstated. Through elected representatives, democracy facilitates public education and awareness on issues affecting individuals and society. That way, the elected representatives could be effective campaigners for the proposed COBE system. Elected representatives will have an added role in educating about the proposed COBE to the uneducated people who constitute a vast majority, especially in the developing countries. If COBE has any merit, won't the political candidates tend, for getting elected, to include the establishment of COBE in their election manifesto?

Democracy, thus, would facilitate publicity to COBE, and this, in turn, would create consensus among people for favoring the establishment of the COBE system.

The following chapter deals with the reforms that could be brought about, under the present capitalism, to the existing forms of the democratic system.

CHAPTER 17

Ultimate Reforms in Democracy under the Existing Capitalism

ONE CAN GIVE THE RIGHT *direction to reformative measures only by visualizing the ultimate system.*

Note:

- Reforms in this section are suggested with an *ultimate democratic order* in mind.
- Since "nations" are the independent or the sovereign units of human societies (and since "world government" has not yet formed), the defects pointed out and reforms suggested here refer to the democratic or political systems of the existing nations.
- These suggestions, however, can readily be extended even to "world government" if such a government is a possibility in the future.
- The defects and reforms mentioned here hold good for all types of democratic nations, irrespective of the nature of the State (unitary or federal), history, wealth, educational level, stage of development, geography, or racial/religious composition.

* Each of these reforms proposed has its merit and can be implemented in isolation. However, since all these reforms are interrelated, each reform works best when employed along with other suggested reforms.

CONTENTS:

I. POLITICAL REFORM—A KEY TO SOCIAL REFORM

Democracy is peculiar to human species. It is the most crucial milestone in the evolution of the political system and is here to stay. There is no question of going back to authoritarian regimes. That is, no nation that is already democratic, even if rudimentarily, would fall back to authoritarianism. All proposals of political reforms in this chapter are, therefore, addressed to further reforms in democracy.

Other significant milestones in the evolution of the political system are the rule of law, political liberalism, constitutional state, separation of the powers into the legislature, executive, and judiciary, representative democracy, parliamentary practice, and so on.

Nevertheless, it is needless to say that many defects still exist in the prevailing political systems. The faults can be seen if one directly observes and analyzes the system itself. The most glaring of all defects is in the process of selection of the policymakers or the politicians.

Many of the politicians that we have come across are politically incompetent, which is compounded by the fact that they lack political will or inclination. They are more known for the promotion of self-interest than of the common good of the people. The derogatory meaning that the word "politics" has come to acquire is because of such politicians. Further, most of the existing political disillusion among the people is due to the same reason. However, the fault is not with the politicians but with the political systems that select them.

Some of the other well-known defects of our political systems have been problems of "party" politics, lack of proportional representation, the influence of money in elections, lack of political participation of the masses, lack of transparency in the political processes, alienation of the masses from the elected representatives, lack of scope for development of politics from grassroots levels, lack of the executive and judiciary autonomy from the legislature, and so on.

In conclusion, political reform is one of the keys to social change. The existing extent of defects in our political systems makes it all the more essential and urgent to bring about political reforms, even if this means making some fundamental changes in the system with the ultimate desirable democratic or political order in mind.

II. Summary of the Proposed Ultimate Democratic System

Basic Assumptions

Political reform is a key to social reform. Along with establishing COBE system, as proposed in this book, bringing political reforms would create more peace and happiness than any other single social change that we can ever think of.

Status of Political Parties

The State would not recognize *political parties*. As political parties are against democratic principles, their existence should not be encouraged statutorily.

Separation of Powers

The legislature should completely be separated from the other two powers. The legislature should be made the head of the State, with executive and judiciary acting as its two arms. Elected leaders or politician should be recruited as legislators; trained civil servants or permanent executives, not political executives, should head the executive.

Posts of king/queen, president, and governors as executive heads, as found in both presidential and parliamentary systems, should be abolished.

The practice of elected representatives/politicians nominating the bureaucratic and judiciary heads should be done away with. Instead, the executive and the judiciary should be made entirely autonomous bodies by bringing about internal democracy in their administration.

Size of Legislative Bodies

The size of the legislative bodies should be kept small and odd-numbered (say, nine) and should be kept the same at all levels of administration.

Multimember Constituency

Each administrative unit is made of a single electoral constituency. Each administrative unit's legislative body should be made multi-membered and small (say, nine-membered), and all the elected members (nine in number) together constitute the legislative body of that administrative unit.

Multiple Voting and Preference Ballot

A voter should be allowed to vote for multiple candidates. The maximum number of candidates that a voter can vote should be the same as the number of seats (nine) present in that constituency/administrative unit's legislative body. The voters should cast the votes by preference ballot. The nine top vote-securing candidates in a constituency should be selected as representatives to the legislative body of that administrative unit.

Voters (Electorates) at Different Administrative Levels — Relay-Election/Representation

Ordinary voting citizen, in this new system, should vote only at the lowest level of administration. Representatives elected at the lowest level, in turn, should elect, among themselves, legislators for the next higher level and so on, till for the highest—that is, at the national level.

"Continuous" Election/Voting

Elections at all levels should be held continuously and not periodically. That is, voters can vote on any day and every day and can change their votes as many times as they would wish. Recruitment or withdrawal of legislators should be made once in (maybe) one month at the lowest administrative units and six months at the higher administrative units. Digital voters' identity cards, computers, and Internet should be made use to take care of any technical difficulties that may arise due to a large number of voters (especially at the lowest level), with each having multiple votes to cast. Online voting could further simplify the election procedure.

The Problem of Upper House

Best results in a group discussion are obtained by making all the talents sit together and not by breaking them into two groups and make them discuss separately. So Lower and the Upper Houses should be merged.

Composition of the Legislative Body — Inner- and Outer-Members

A legislative body will have the properly elected as the true legislators. Let us call these members, for convenience, the core or *inner-members*. The inner-members will be nine in number, as decided earlier. The legislative body should also consist of other members, the *outer-members*, to assist the inner-members in the task of legislation and to serve as a "check" or "opposition" on the performances of the inner-members.

The legislative body of an administrative unit of a given level, other than the lowest, should have all the inner-members of the immediately lower constituent administrative units as part of the total outer-members (legislative outer-members). The outer-members should also include heads of several branches of the executive (bureaucrats) and the judiciary. Few more of the outer-members should be nominated by votes, by the inner-members. Thus, a legislative body would consist of the *inner-members* and *four* types of *outer-members*.

MAXIMUM SIZE OF A LEGISLATIVE BODY

The size of a legislative body, including the outer-members, should not be too big. The legislative outer-members will make up the largest part (nine multiplied by the number of constituent lower administrative units) of a legislative body. The number of legislative outer-members for the administrative units of the lowest level would not be fixed. It would include the candidates who have not made it to the inner-members and any freshly registered legislative aspirants, both of which are variable.

OPTIMUM NUMBER OF DIVISION OF AN ADMINISTRATIVE UNIT HIGHER THAN THE LOWEST

The administrative units of a nation at all levels, except the lowest, should be made up of or divided into *five* immediately lower-level administrative units. In other words, each administrative unit should be made up of *five* subunits. That is, a nation should be made up of *five* states; a state should be made up of *five* districts; and so on.

Number of Levels or Tiers of Administration in a Nation

The number of tiers of administration a nation would have will be the number of times the nation's population is divided successively by *five* (number of division of an administrative unit) until a figure less than twenty thousand is arrived at. To illustrate this further, suppose the population of a nation is one million. The number of administrative tiers that this nation would have will be *three*. That is, the nation would be divided into a first division—*states*, second division—*districts*, and third division—*wards* or whatever the name is assigned to a division/tier.

Functional Differentiation of Inner-Members and Outer-Members in the Legislative House

Since the inner-members are the true representatives of people, they must have all the rights of legislation: 1) *right to participate in the legislative discussion* (legislative initiation), 2) *voting rights* (in policy-making and the election of the legislative body of the next higher level, as in the newly proposed political system), and 3) *right to become the speaker.* However, the outer-members would have only the *right to participate in legislative discussions* (legislative initiation).

To Provide for the Dual Functions of the Elected Legislators at Two Nearby Levels of Administrative Units

At a given administrative unit, if the inner-members have legislative sessions in one week, for instance, the next week they would attend the legislative sessions as legislative outer-members in the immediately higher administrative unit, and the week after, they, as inner-members, would have a legislative session again at their own administrative level, and so on. That is, legislators will attend their legislative sessions at different administrative levels as inner- and outer-members every alternate week.

WORK SCHEDULE OF LEGISLATORS

Four-days–a-week legislative sessions might be ideal. The rest *three* days could be used both for *fieldwork* and as a *break/holiday*. At the highest administrative level/national level, however, legislators would have *four-days-a-week* legislative sessions in one week and no legislative session in the week after, as there will not be an administrative unit higher than the national level. Therefore, the national-level legislators would have *four* days in one week for legislative sessions and all the *seven* days in the next week for *work related to foreign affairs, fieldwork*, and a break/holiday.

ASSESSMENT OF PERFORMANCE OF LEGISLATORS BY THE VOTERS — LIVE TELECAST OF LEGISLATIVE SESSIONS

Voters need to assess the performance of the legislators continuously. So it is vital that all the legislative sessions at all levels of administration must be telecast for the voters, including the ordinary voters at the lowest administrative units.

MOVEMENT OF LEGISLATORS — WITHIN A LEGISLATIVE BODY AND BETWEEN DIFFERENT LEVELS

The movement of legislators due to change in votes is periodical (once in a month for the legislators of the lowest level and once in six months for those of the higher levels), as previously suggested. Within a legislative body, a legislative outer-member, thus, can anytime move, periodically, up the ladder and replace an inner-member who, meanwhile, moves down to become the legislative outer-member. An inner-member can also move up to become an inner-member of the legislative body of the higher level. Conversely, an inner-member, of other than the lowest level, can move down and back to their lower level where they become the inner-member again. Should that happen, the member at the bottom of the inner-members at that level would move down to become the inner-member of the immediately lower level.

STATE FUNDING OF ELECTION CAMPAIGNS

Election campaigns should be State-funded, and the funding should be total in the sense that the State itself should arrange for the various means of the campaign. Campaigning by means other than what is organized by the State should be made illegal. Election campaigns of all the parties and even the independents should be funded.

SECRET OR OPEN BALLOT?

Legislators, if not the common voters, should cast their votes by open ballot.

LEGISLATIVE BODIES AT LOWER ADMINISTRATIVE LEVELS

Full-fledged legislative bodies should be set up at all levels of administration, including the lowermost.

FUNCTIONS OF THE LEGISLATURE

There would be no divide in this setup of the legislature into "ruling" and "opposition."

The legislative body, in this new system, would have essentially two functions: 1) legislation and 2) voting for the election of the legislative body of the immediately higher administrative unit. Obviously, the second function would not be there for the highest legislative body—that is, at the national level. The legislative bodies would perform mainly only these functions and all these functions should be performed only within legislative sessions and nowhere else.

ELECTION OF THE SPEAKER

The speaker should be elected, among and by the members, by continuous voting where the members should vote anybody other than themself. The results of the voting are freshly effective for each legislative session.

FUNCTIONS OF SPEAKER

In addition to being the moderator, the speaker should retain the functions of discussion and voting as well, unlike in many of the existing systems.

EMOLUMENTS AND SERVICE CONDITIONS OF LEGISLATORS

The emoluments and service condition of legislators should be generous and liberal.

DEALING FURTHER BLOWS TO PARTY POLITICS

The State does not recognize any political party. Therefore, there should be no legal sanction for "party-whip" or anti-defection measures.

A candidate should be allowed to mention their party affiliation if any.

Election symbols, if needed, should be given to individual candidates and not to political parties.

POLITICAL EDUCATION AND PARTICIPATION OF THE MASSES IN THE POLITICAL PROCESSES

The function of political education of the masses should be entrusted with an autonomous body—the Election Commission. Some of the essential tasks that the commission should undertake are the introduction of political education at early schooling, encouraging nongovernmental, voluntary political organizations to take up the cause of political education of the masses, arranging political campaigns of candidates, making the proceedings of legislative sessions public through various media, and so on.

MAKING EXECUTIVE AND JUDICIARY AUTONOMOUS BY BRINGING INTERNAL DEMOCRACY IN THEIR ADMINISTRATIONS

In the existing democracies, both the executive and the judiciary heads are nominated by the legislators. That takes away much of the independence of the executive and the judiciary regarding their administrative decision-making and puts them at the mercy of the legislature. Autonomy can be achieved by bringing internal democracy in their administration. The form of democracy they need to adopt could be on the lines of what is proposed for the legislature.

Transition to the New System from the Existing Ones

Transition to the new democratic system should involve, at least, two measures: 1) educating the masses about the new system by an autonomous Election Commission and 2) relocating the existing political leaders or legislators to the new system.

All existing legislators, whatever their present level (national, state, and so on), should first contest the election at the lowest level for the local legislative body and then get elected for higher level/s as it would be a "relay election or representation" in the new system.

The transition of the executive and the judiciary to the proposed new model would be similar to that of the legislature.

Defects in the Existing Political Systems and Suggestions for Reform

* Basic Assumptions
* The Three Powers—Legislature, Executive, and the Judiciary
* Constituting Legislative Bodies or Electoral Reform
* The Legislature—Function, Powers, and Procedures
* Dealing Further Blows to Party Politics

* Political Education and Participation of the Masses in the Political Processes
* Making Executive and Judiciary Autonomous by Bringing Internal Democracy in Their Administrations

BASIC ASSUMPTIONS

* Divisions of Governance or Administration
* Unitary or Federal State?
* No-Party Politics

DIVISIONS OF GOVERNANCE OR ADMINISTRATION

For effective administration, the government of a nation is divided both territorially and functionally.

Territorially, the government is divided into smaller administrative units—the extent of division mainly decided by the size of the population. The best way of a territorial division is by tier system—that is, dividing in a simple hierarchical order. It means that the whole nation is taken as one single administrative unit at the highest level; the nation is divided into "states" (the first-division administrative units), states into "districts" (the second-division administrative units), and so on.

Functionally, the government is divided at each regional level into three organs or powers: the legislature, the executive, and the judiciary. The legislature is the law-making body, the executive executes or administers the law, and the judiciary interprets the law and enforces it.

Unitary or Federal State?

A *unitary State* is the one in which we find the exercise of supreme legislative authority by one central power. In contrast, a *federal State* is a political contrivance intended to reconcile national unity and power for which the legislative authority is divided between central or federal power and smaller units.

Neither the unitary nor the federal principles can be said to be better or worse than the other. Moreover, neither can necessarily fit all given situations. In general, one or the other is chosen because it is considered more appropriate to the particular case. The unitary principle has usually been adopted where there is a reasonable degree of homogeneity in the population. The federal type of constitution has been adopted by nations having broad diversity—geographically, culturally, politically, or on the grounds of race, color, or creed.

The federal type allows a great deal of legislative experimentation. In contrast, the unitary one is advantageous in that it is simplified, and there is no waste of legislative repetition. Thus, federalism is indicated for integrating a heterogeneous population into a nation. However, assuming that all populations would move from heterogeneity to homogeneity in the long run, so should the State move from federal type to, ultimately, unitary one—to take full advantage of the unitary system. At the same time, nations, which are already under a unitary system, should be responsive to possible conflicts between the center and the constituent smaller units, in which case it should not hesitate to delegate legislative powers to the latter.

No-Party Politics

Sooner the party breaks the better—Jane Austin (novelist).

However, the State, at the same time, cannot ban political parties, which is against the democratic principle of freedom to form an association.

The principal need for the existence of political parties, it is argued, is for crystallizing the opinions of common people on critical national issues. However, what we see, on the contrary, is that party propaganda rouses false spirit in people and divides not only the legislature but the country into rival camps. That nullifies democracy and, thereby, also hinders the development of the nation.

It is known that whereas parliament discusses, the parties decide. Even within a party, because of the "party-whip" (which is in practice in some political systems), legislators lose their free will and independent thinking in the matters of policymaking. Legislation or politics, then, would be more "party" based than "issue" based. Besides, able persons are kept out of government, even if they get elected, because they are not members of a popular party, and incompetents may get elected because they are members of such a party. All that a voter requires to know before voting is the political competence of the individual candidate, not what party they are in. In any case, one sees little difference in the essence of the rival parties' manifestos, especially for the majority who are economically backward.

The party system has nothing to be commended about. It evolved into existence and continues to exist because of many defects that have been there in the democratic or political systems. It has stayed with us for a long time, and we have taken it for granted as an inevitable and even indispensable part of our political system.

Thus, a two-party government is better than an one-party government (dictatorship); a multi-party government is better than a two-party government; the best is a no-party government.

Nevertheless, it should be stressed that nongovernmental, voluntary political organizations, and not political parties, could still have roles to play in the political processes, most important of which is the political education of the masses. (See "Political Education and Participation of the Masses.")

In conclusion—the State, in principle, cannot recognize political parties. At the same time, it cannot ban them either, as the fundamental freedom of a citizen to associate for all purposes, including political, cannot be taken away. All measures to mitigate the evils of the party system, therefore, should be addressed indirectly, which is by reforming the political system. Factors acting as the cause for or necessitating a need for the existence of political parties are traceable to specific defects in the prevailing political systems. These are considered in the following sections.

THE THREE POWERS—LEGISLATURE, EXECUTIVE, AND THE JUDICIARY

* Separation of Powers
* Who Should Head the State—Legislature, Executive, or Judiciary?
* Whom to Choose for the Three Powers?
* Who Selects Whom?

SEPARATION OF POWERS

Originally the king was the lawmaker, the executor of the law, and the judge. However, as the business of the State increased, both in amount and complexity, there grew a need for a convenient means of coping with this. As a result of this and the advent of democracy, there evolved the normal social process of specialization of function or division of labor and, therefore, a tendency to delegate these powers of the monarchy. That resulted in the division of government or administration into three departments—legislature, executive, and the judiciary.

However, the basis of democracy and political and public liberty rests not only in the convenient specialization of these functions but their absolute separation in different hands. Montesquieu (an 18th century political philosopher) concluded that "wherever the right of making and executing the law is vested in the same man or one and the only body of men, there can be no public liberty, because of the danger that the same monarch or the senate could enact tyrannical laws and execute them in a tyrannical manner."

Though these principles are well accepted, they are not fully appreciated by present democracies, whether following parliamentary or presidential systems.

In parliamentary democracies like India and the United Kingdom, for example, the Cabinet (of ministers) that is constituted out of the elected legislature is the executive head (head of ministries). It, thus, performs both legislative and executive functions. This lack of legislature's differentiation into a pure policymaking organ would mean (in addition to the danger of tyranny, as pointed out by Montesquieu) that executive functions consume part of its time—to the neglect of its policymaking function. In the interrogation of these legislator-cum-executives, parliaments in UK and India consume a considerable portion of their time on their executive performances.

In the presidential system (e.g., the United States), unlike the parliamentary system, the executive head (president) is not drawn from the legislature. Separate elections elect the president and the legislature. In that sense, therefore, it can be said that the presidential system achieves a higher degree of separation of powers than the parliamentary system. Nevertheless, as executive head, the president enjoys extensive legislative power, which is co-extensive with the legislature. Considered that way, therefore, even the presidential system has failed in separating the powers.

WHO SHOULD HEAD THE STATE—LEGISLATURE, EXECUTIVE, OR THE JUDICIARY?

Logically, lawmaking precedes its execution, interpretation, and enforcement. Besides, only lawmaking is an active process, and others are passive. Therefore, the legislature is of greater importance than the executive, which administers the law, or the judiciary, which enforces it. The legislature is concerned throughout with the problems of the people and nation. It gauges public opinion and aspirations, expresses their sovereign will as laws, and thus determines their destiny. Hence among the three organs of government, the legislature occupies the prime place.

From all that is said above, it is clear that the legislature should be the head of the state, with the executive and judiciary just acting as its two arms.

The legislation, as we understand it today, is a comparatively recent development. In the earliest democratic political societies, the elected representatives performed only the executive duty. They sought to evade the responsibility of legislation, wishing to leave it, in effect, to the king, who had always performed it. In modern governments, the importance of the legislative function has dramatically increased in proportion to the rise of democracy. The legislative organ has gained a new democratic significance. That is because of the growing political conscious-ness of the mass of the people in whose collective interest laws are passed. In practice, however, the legislative organ is yet to receive the importance it deserves. For, in both parliamentary and presidential systems, the executive head, not the legislature, is also the head of the state.

Whom to Choose for the Three Powers?

Agreeing that the ideal is to provide for specialization of func-tion, and at the same time, to entrust the responsibilities in three different hands, the question now arises: Whom to choose for each of the three powers?

Since people are the masters of their own destiny in democ-racy, the legislature is to be constituted by popularly elected representatives or politicians who need not be professional administrators or experts in any field. On the other hand, the executive and judiciary, which involve purely specialist func-tions, are to be constituted by trained civil servants or profes-sionals. A popularly elected representative, being an amateur, should not try to run the executive business at which civil ser-vants are experts. In a democracy, therefore, the legislature con-stitutes the political system. In contrast, the other two parts of the government, executive and judiciary, do not.

The practice of recruiting elected leaders as the executive heads can create scope for political corruption and scandal. Politicians and businesspersons or corporates, for example, tend to form an unethical nexus between them, with the former favoring the latter's business interests by misuse of executive powers and the latter favoring the former with monetary and other benefits. Politicians (elected representatives) retaining executive powers may partly be the cause for the rise of two evils, namely, political corruption and "party politics". Given the amount of (illegal) money and other benefits in executive posts in this system, the candidates tend to go to the extent of forming or joining "parties"—the political parties. They stand more chances of winning elections and forming the government when they are organized into a party than when they do it as independents.

Both parliamentary and presidential systems are guilty of not following the above principle. In both these systems, lay representatives, not professionals, head the executive. The reason for this seemingly obvious anomaly in both parliamentary and presidential systems is not hard to find. It could be that the elected leaders are reluctant to relinquish the executive power, partly because of the hangover from the earlier era of monarchy or dictatorship and also because the ruling class finds the executive powers expedient in meeting personal interests. Hence the peculiar prevailing situation: the elected leaders retain executive powers and, at the same time, head the state.

Besides, in a parliamentary system, the existence of titular/nominal executive heads—the queen in the UK, president, and governors in India—is not only redundant but a source for further confusion.

WHO SELECTS WHOM?

The legislature is that part of the government that assesses the people's opinions and aspirations, translates them into laws, and thus determines their destiny. In democracy, since the government is ultimately responsible for its actions to the public, it is but natural that the common people should select (by election) the legislature.

However, since the executive (and the judiciary) involves specialist functions, common citizens, not being competent to judge the executive performances, should not be used to elect the executive. Neither the elected representative, for the same reason, should be used to select the executive. Therefore, it is not acceptable if the president (executive head) is elected by the laypeople, as in the presidential system, or if the prime minister (the chief executive) is elected by the legislators (lay representatives), as in the parliamentary system.

While agreeing that professionals should head the executive or bureaucracy and the judiciary, the question remains as to who should select these heads.

In the existing political systems, the political executives— the cabinet in the parliamentary system and the president in the presidential system—recruit the top of the permanent executives and the judiciary by nomination. However, the political executives who are elected representatives are not competent themselves to judge the competence of the professionals. This practice of nomination is the primary cause for keeping the bureaucracy and judiciary at the mercy of politicians. For complete separation of the powers or rather, for delinking bureaucracy and judiciary from politics, therefore, yet another vital step would be the abandonment of the practice of nomination of bureaucratic and judiciary heads by the elected representatives. A question arises, then: What would be the system for the administration of the executive and the judiciary? The solution may be to make them fully autonomous. The executive and the judiciary could be made independent by bringing about internal democracy or election in their administration. The form of democracy to be adopted in the executive and judiciary could be on the lines of the proposed reforms for the legislature in the following sections. (See also "Making Executive and Judiciary Autonomous by Bringing Internal Democracy in Their Administrations.")

Thus, in conclusion, the following measures must be taken to completely rectify the three powers in the matters of their functional interrelation and selection of personnel. The legislature is made the head of the state, with executive and judiciary acting as its two arms.

* The legislature is completely separated from the other two powers. Elected leaders/politicians are made legislators; trained civil servants or permanent executives, not political executives, head the executive.
* Posts of king/queen, president, and governors as executive heads in both presidential and parliamentary systems are abolished.
* Doing away with the practice of elected representatives/ politicians nominating the bureaucratic and judiciary heads and instead, making the executive and the judiciary completely autonomous by bringing about internal democracy in their administration.

CONSTITUTING LEGISLATIVE BODIES OR ELECTORAL REFORM

* Size of Legislative Bodies
* Multimember Constituency
* Multiple Voting and Preference Ballot
* Voters (Electorates) at Different Administrative Levels and Relay-Election/Representation

* "Continuous" Election/Voting
* The Problem of Upper House
* Composition of the Legislative Body—Inner- and Outer-members
* Maximum Size of a Legislative Body
* Optimum Number of Division of an Administrative Unit Higher Than the Lowest
* Number of Levels or Tiers of Administration in a Nation
* Functional Differentiation of Inner-members and Outer-members in the Legislative House
* To Provide for the Dual Functions of the Elected Legislators at Two Nearby Levels of Administrative Units
* Work Schedule of Legislators
* Assessment of Performance of Legislators by the Voters—Live Telecast of Legislative Sessions
* Movement of Legislators—Within a Legislative Body and between Different Levels
* State Funding of Election Campaigns
* Secret or Open Ballot?
* Legislative Bodies at Lower Administrative Levels
* Some Conclusions

Size of Legislative Bodies

One crucial factor that decides the efficiency of a legislative body in decision making is its size—that is, the number of members in it. So let us consider what should be the ideal size of a legislative body.

Any population can be conceived as being made up of several overlapping groups of different interests and opinions. In the making of any policy, therefore, all these interests and opinions should be well represented. Since one person, as a rule, is not able to do this effectively, it follows that the legislature should be a multimember body. At the same time, the size should not be too big, lest it prevents speedy decision making and meaningful participation of every member. Countries with the presidential system have decision-making powers concentrated more at the hands of a single individual, president, at the national level (since the legislative powers of the president are co-extensive with those of the legislature). Those having a parliamentary system (e.g., India, UK) usually have huge legislative bodies.

Once it is decided that the number should neither be one nor be hundreds, a question arises: What, then, is the optimum or ideal size of a legislative body. Any number around ten should be ideal, as it is more than what is needed for representing the diverse interests and opinions existing in a society and, at the same time, not too large to prevent the meaningful participation of each member or speedy decision-making. However, it has to be an odd number so as to get clear-cut voting verdicts in the matters of policy-making or speaker's election. It could be either *nine or eleven.* For our discussion purposes, let us assume that the elected legislative body should be *nine-membered* for optimum size. However, the more exact number can be arrived at only after some trial and error. Also, the size of the legislative body should be the same at all levels of administration since the number of types of interests and opinions existing in a population is more or less the same regardless of its size.

Multimember Constituency

Having fixed the number of legislators for the legislative body at each administrative unit, let us move on to see how to get this number by election.

The usual constituency arrangement has been by the division of an administrative unit at each level into many smaller territorial electoral constituencies, with each returning a single member, or at most, two members. The highest vote-securing candidate would be selected as the legislative member—the so-called first-past-the-post method. However, a sole representative is not sufficient, as discussed before, to represent the diverse interests and opinions that are there both across the population and within each individual. That is, in this system, minority interests and views are not represented in policy-making. Further, it is a common knowledge that votes garnered by a winning candidate, even if they win with a large margin, would rarely be more than 40 percent of the total cast in their constituency. Thus, the remaining 60 percent of the voters go unrepresented. Another significant drawback of constituting a legislative body by breaking the unit into smaller constituencies is that candidates tend to become regionally biased, whether in promising the voters or, if elected, in performing legislative functions. These aspects make the representation not only insufficient but disproportional. In addition to being directly disadvantageous, disproportional representation could also favor the rise of another menace, namely, the party system. One more drawback of a single-member constituency is that a candidate who is placed second, by votes, in one constituency might do better, in terms of getting votes, than several other candidates who are placed first in other constituencies. That is, there is no guarantee in the existing system that all the winning candidates are the toppers of that administrative unit.

Further, the size of the legislative bodies constituted by breaking an administrative unit into smaller constituencies would depend on the population of that administrative unit.

That means that the size of legislative bodies at national and state levels will be huge.

Thus, making an administrative unit a single constituency and electing several representatives from it has many advantages. It ensures *proportional representation* (PR), all the elected would be toppers of the administrative unit, and it discourages party politics.

Multiple Voting and Preference Ballot

If an electoral constituency is multi-membered, each voter, then, would have the right to have a say in the selection of every member of the legislative body. For this reason and also to enable to get a large number of representatives from a single constituency, a voter should be allowed to vote for multiple candidates. Also, the maximum number of candidates that a voter can vote should be the same as the number of seats present in that constituency's or administrative unit's legislative body. That is, the voter should be allowed to vote for up to nine candidates (if legislative bodies are nine-membered). The nine top vote-securing candidates in a constituency would then be selected as representatives of that administrative unit's legislative body.

Besides, the ballot will have to be a "preference ballot." That is, a voter is allowed to rank his first choice, second choice, third, and so on up to nine. Voters rank the candidates as many as they care to, but it should be taken care that they are in the full knowledge that more a ballot is complete, the more effective would it be. This kind of ballot would be fair for the voters and the candidates, as well, as it recognizes many gradations and subtleties in opinions or priorities of the voters.

Voters (Electorates) at Different Administrative Levels and Relay-Election/Representation

What is in practice, generally, is that the ordinary voting citizens directly elect the representatives for all the levels of administration. However, the average citizens are better able to relate their problems with those of their locality than with their state, nation, and so on. So, they would do more justice, as voters, if their voting were restricted to their local government's election. This voting restriction would also spare them the hardships of voting several times at various levels. Moreover, the need for crystallizing the opinions of common people on state or national issues, and therefore, also the need for the existence of political parties is minimized in this proposed new system, since most of what the common people need knowing, as far as voting is concerned, are the issues of their locality.

Therefore, the ordinary voting citizen should vote only at the lowest level of administration.

Who, then, would elect legislators for the higher levels?

The representatives elected at the lowest level should, in turn, elect among themselves, legislators for the next higher level and so on, till the highest—that is, the national, level. This scheme can be extended when the condition becomes ripe, even to form "world government." In such a system, representation at the lowest level would be direct and at the higher levels more indirect. So, election or representation in such a system would be a sort of relay-election or relay-representation.

To illustrate this further: suppose a nation is organized into three levels of administration—district, state, and nation. Common citizens elect the district legislators, nine in number, as proposed earlier, for their respective districts; all the district legislators of a state (nine multiplied by the number of districts in the state) would elect among themselves, nine state legislators; all the state legislators of the country (nine multiplied by the number of states in the country) would then elect among themselves, nine national legislators. In this illustration, thus, a district legislator who is the local legislator is the people's representative, a state legislator is the people's representatives' representative, and a national legislator is people's representatives' representatives' representative. In yet other words, common citizens constitute the *electoral college* (a body of voters) for the election of the legislative body at the lowest level—the district level, all the district-level legislators of a state would constitute the *electoral college* for the election of state legislators, and so on. All the legislators, thus, except the national level, in addition to their legislative functions at their level, would also have the function of electing legislators for the next higher level. A candidate, thus, aiming at the legislative office of a higher level should have earlier won through all the elections at the lower levels. Besides, any legislator of a higher level, in this system, who fails to get reelected for that level, would automatically fall to the legislative body of the next lower level.

However, since the size of the electoral college at all levels except the lowest, in this new system, would be small, for getting meaningful results, a legislator at any level should vote anybody other than oneself.

Apart from the advantage that right people would vote at each level of administration in the election of legislators, this new method would establish, for legislative bodies of different levels, a smooth continuum both for recruitment of legislators and for legislative interaction. Furthermore, this method would be an inbuilt way of eliminating the nonserious contenders at all levels except maybe the lowest. Another very significant advantage of this electoral reform would be its simplicity. One of the benefits, in turn, of being simple is that all people, including ordinary voters, can easily understand, follow, and participate in the political processes, making the system more successful. Besides, since only campaigning to the ordinary citizens entails much cost for candidates—in terms of time, energy, and money, this new system would make the political campaigning easy and economical for electing legislative bodies at all levels except maybe the lowest. Reduction of costs, in turn, makes it feasible for the introduction of yet another vital electoral reform, namely, State funding of election campaigns (dealt in a subsequent section).

"Continuous" Election/Voting
How often the elections have to be held?

The practice everywhere is the periodical election—once in four or five years. The major drawback of this is that candidates once elected cannot be recalled until the next elections even if the voters realize later that the performances of the representatives are not up to the mark. Another problem is that often the composition of the legislative body might change drastically and suddenly soon after the elections, rendering the system unstable. One more drawback is that all the voters can't be available on a single day—the polling day, preventing the participation of many.

An alternative, without the drawbacks of a periodical election, would be by what can be called "continuous election/voting." By this, it means that polling should not be confined to a single day but should be held continuously on any and every day and as and when the voters feel like voting or changing their votes. That is, there should be provision for voters to vote on any day and change their votes any number of times. For this, the polling booth should be open and available continuously throughout the year, just like a post office. This system goes well with the natural tendency of voters who always keep a continuous vigil on the performances of their representatives. However, it would be more practical, especially in other than the local level, if counting of votes and announcement of results, and accordingly, recruitment or withdrawal of legislators is done on a less continuous basis. The minimum term of a legislator could be fixed as *six* months. Terms of lesser duration are not practical as the change of an administrative level for a legislator, which is a possibility in the proposed new political system, as explained before, also involves the hardships of moving of the residence of the legislators along with their family from one place to another. The minimum term of a legislator at the local level, the lowest level of administration, could be fixed as *one* month.

This method of continuous voting can easily be employed for the election of legislators at all higher levels, as the voters involved in these are legislators themselves whose job as a legislator would be full time. Also, they will be small in number and politically more mature than the average citizen. However, there can be difficulties in making the ordinary citizens adapt to this continuous voting method. There can also be technical difficulties in registering the votes because the common voters are in large numbers. These difficulties can easily be overcome if digital voter's identity cards, computers, and the internet are made use of. Online voting could further simplify the election procedure.

Thus, a continuous election is advantageous in that elected members who are not performing can be recalled; change of composition of the legislative bodies would be gradual, rendering continuity and therefore, also, stability to legislative bodies. It enables more people to participate in elections. In addition, because of its potential to recall legislators, this method of continuous voting, working along with "relay-representation" proposed earlier, acts as a continuous internal check against nonperformance, irregularities, autocratic behavior, or any other misconduct of legislators—minimizing the need for any other form of a check.

THE PROBLEM OF UPPER HOUSE

The primary reason for the need for an Upper House or Second Chamber is for acting as a "check" for the functioning of the Lower House that is constituted by popularly elected representatives. Another reason is that many politically talented people cannot contest the elections because of their professional commitments. More commonly, they cannot stand the roughs and toughs of the elections because of their soft nature or weak constitution (old age or sickness). How to make the best of these talents? To provide for these needs, most countries have Upper House or Second Chamber that is in addition to and independent of the Lower House or the First Chamber. However, the main objection to this arrangement is that the best results in a group discussion are obtained by making all the talents sit together, not by breaking them into two groups and making them discuss separately. Besides, this separation and also the fact that the Upper House is subordinate to the Lower regarding decision-making have rendered the former mostly redundant. Moreover, having two houses is a waste of time and other resources. However, it is quite understandable for countries like India and the UK to have two Houses, as the numbers of members in both the Houses are too big to allow any merging, in the existing system.

COMPOSITION OF THE LEGISLATIVE BODY—INNER- AND OUTER-MEMBERS

A legislative body will have the properly elected as the true legislators. Let us call these members, for convenience, the core or *inner-members*. The inner-members will be nine in number, as decided earlier. The legislative body should also consist of other members to assist the inner-members in the task of legislation and to serve as a "check" or "opposition" on the performances of the inner-members. Let us call these other members, for convenience, the *outer-members*.

Who will all be the outer-members?

Because this new model will have *relay-representation* and *continuous voting,* the legislative body of an administrative unit of a given level, other than the lowest, should have all the inner-members of the immediately lower constituent administrative units as part of the total outer-members. Let us call these members *legislative outer-members.* The outer-members should also include heads of several branches of the executive (bureaucrats) and the judiciary. Let us call these *executive outer-members* and *judiciary outer-members,* respectively. The outer-members from the executive and the judiciary will be of help to the inner-members as consultants while formulating legislation. Also, they serve as a source for legislative initiation. Besides, this arrangement helps to connect the legislature with the executive and the judiciary. Few more of the outer-members should be nominated by votes, by the inner-members. The nominated ones are the equivalents of the Upper House members of the existing systems and can be composed of people like retired judges, executives, scientists, social scientists, economists, diplomats, and social activists who are persons of eminence in their fields. Let us call these members *eminent outer-members.* Thus, a legislative body would consist of the *inner-members* and *four* types of outer-members—*legislative outer-members, executive outer-members, judiciary outer-members,* and *eminent outer-members.*

At the lowest-level administrative units, the legislative outer-members will be those candidates who have not made it to the inner-members. It will also include any freshly registered legislator aspirants.

MAXIMUM SIZE OF A LEGISLATIVE BODY

The size of a legislative body should not be too big, lest it prevents speedy decision-making and meaningful participation of every member. A legislative body would consist of *nine* inner-members and four types of outer-members—legislative outer-members, executive outer-members, judiciary outer-members, and eminent outer-members. Among these, the number of the legislative outer-members would be the largest as it includes nine inner-members from each of the constituent administrative units of the immediately lower level. So the number of legislative outer-members would be nine multiplied by the number of divisions in the immediately lower administrative units. To keep the number of legislative outer-members small, the number of divisions that an administrative unit, other than the lowest, is required to be small. If an administrative unit, other than the lowest, is divided into *five* constituent immediately lower-level administrative units, then the number of legislative outer-members for that administrative unit would be *nine* multiplied by *five, forty-five.* Now, let the number of executive outer-members, judiciary outer-members, and eminent outer-members be *six, two, and two,* respectively (total *ten*), so the total number of outer-members would be *fifty-five.* The total number of legislators, inner and outer, would be *nine* plus *fifty-five*—that is, *sixty-four,* which is not too big in terms of conducting legislative sessions effectively.

The number of legislative outer-members for the lowest-level administrative units would not be fixed as it would include the candidates who have not made it to the inner-members and any freshly registered legislator aspirants, both of which are variable.

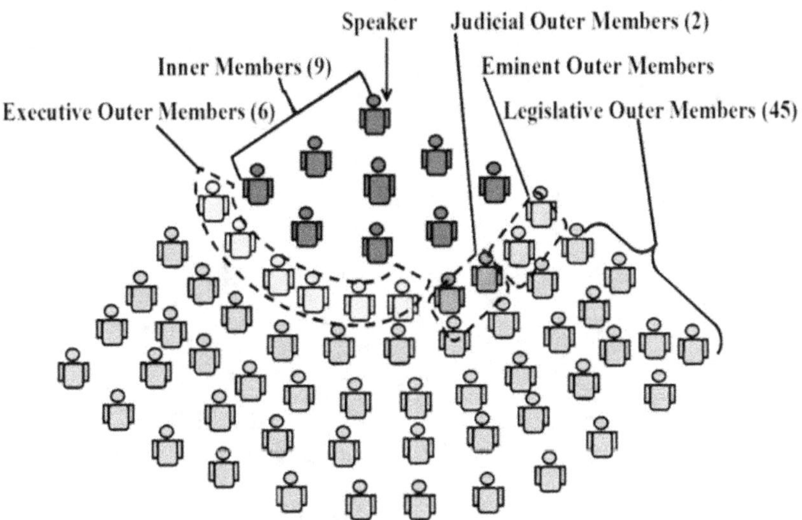

Figure 3: Composition of the legislative body

OPTIMUM NUMBER OF DIVISION OF AN ADMINISTRATIVE UNIT HIGHER THAN THE LOWEST

As discussed above, to keep the size of the legislative bodies not too big, it becomes mandatory that administrative units at each level, except of course the lowest, be divided into not more than *five* lower administrative units. At the same time, if the administrative units are divided into numbers less than *five,* then a nation needs to be divided territorially into too many administrative levels or tiers, which would necessitate having too many legislative bodies.

Thus, the administrative units of a nation at all levels, except the lowest, should be made up of or divided into *five* immediately lower-level administrative units. That is, each administrative unit should be made up of *five* subunits. To illustrate it further: a nation should be made up of *five* states; a state should be made up of *five* districts; and so on.

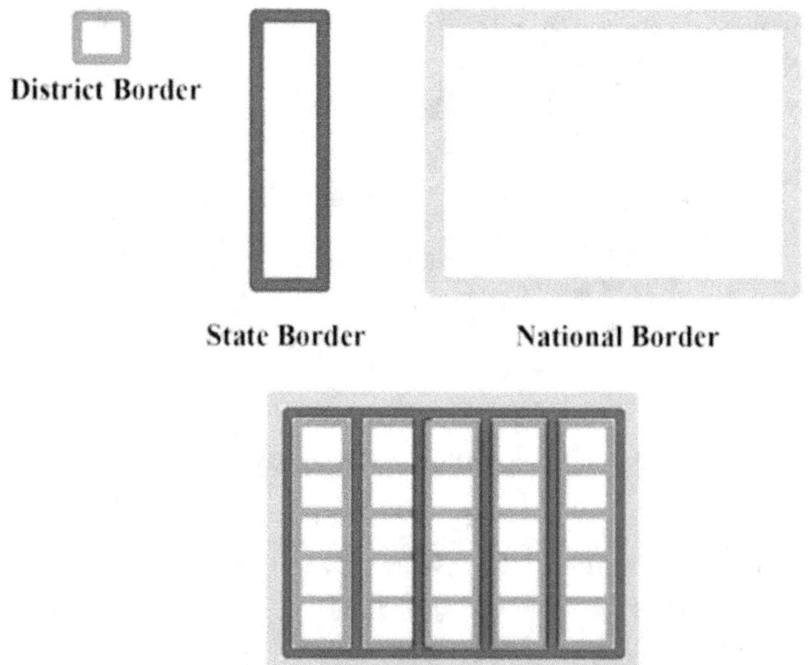

Figure 4: Schematic representation of the territorial division of a nation for administration

(Note: Nation is territorially divided at two levels—state and district.)

NUMBER OF LEVELS OR TIERS OF ADMINISTRATION IN A NATION
Given that each administrative unit, other than the lowest, should be made up of *five* subunits as decided above, the number of levels or tiers that a nation should have, depends on 1) the population size of the nation and 2) the maximum population that the lowest administrative unit can have. Let us fix the maximum population size to be allowed for the lowest administrative unit at twenty thousand. Then the number of tiers of administration a nation would have will be the number of times the population of the nation is divided successively by *five* (number of division of an administrative unit) until a figure less than twenty thousand is arrived at. To illustrate, suppose the population of a nation is one million. The number of administrative tiers that this nation would have will be *three*. That is, the nation would be divided into a first division—*states*, second division—*districts*, and third division—*wards* or whatever the name is assigned to a division or tier. India, the population of which is 1.3 billion, would have, for example, a *seven*-tier division. The names for these, from the first division to the seventh, could be the *superstate, state, substate, superdistrict, district, subdistrict,* and *ward*. If the maximum population size to be allowed for the lowest administrative unit is one hundred thousand, instead of twenty thousand, then the nation would have one less level of administrative division.

FUNCTIONAL DIFFERENTIATION OF INNER-MEMBERS AND
OUTER-MEMBERS IN THE LEGISLATIVE HOUSE
The act of legislation, to be sure, should involve setting up of social goals, assessment of the problems of the people or region in attaining these goals, and then, formulation of legislation or policies to solve these problems. For this, the members of the body should

first exchange views (discuss or deliberate) about the desired social goals, existing issues, and possible legislative measures to solve them—all of which constitute *legislative initiation*. Then it should decide, by voting, which particular legislation is to be adopted. Though technically it is the legislature (inner-members, in the proposed system), which ultimately decides on a policy by voting, the outer-members can be a good source for legislative initiation.

Since the inner-members are the true representatives of people, they must have all the rights of legislation:

1) *right to participate in the legislative discussion* (legislative initiation),

2) *voting rights* (in policy-making and the election of the legislative body of the next higher level, as in the newly proposed political system)

3) *right to become the speaker.*

However, the outer-members would have only *right to participate in legislative discussions* (legislative initiation). In other words, the outer-members can influence the legislation only by way of discussion. However, they cannot vote or become the speaker.

To Provide for the Dual Functions of the Elected Legislators at Two Nearby Levels of Administrative Units

As proposed in the new system, an elected representative will have dual functions, except at the highest (national) level: 1) as the inner-member at his or her administrative level and 2) as the legislative outer-member in the immediately higher level. Inner-members at the national level, however, have the additional work related to *foreign affairs.* This dual role necessitates allotting different times for legislative functions of administrative units that are at different levels but are at nearby levels. At a given administrative unit, if the inner-members have legislative sessions in one week, for instance, the next week, they would attend the legislative sessions as legislative outer-members in the immediately higher administrative unit. The week after, they, as inner-members, would have a legislative session again at their administrative level, and so on. In other words, the inner-members of an administrative unit will attend legislative sessions, at their level as inner-members and the immediately higher level as legislative outer-members, in alternate weeks. To illustrate further, suppose a nation is divided into *states* and *districts*. Then there are *three* administrative levels—district level, state level, and national level. Which level functions in what capacity in a timeline of four weeks—week 1, week 2, week 3, and week 4—is shown below.

Administrative Level	Week 1	Week 2	Week 3	Week 4
District Level	As inner-members at the district level	As legislative outer-members at the state level	As inner-members at the district level	As legislative outer-members at the state level
State Level	As legislative outer-members at the national level	As inner-members at the state level	As legislative outer-members at the national level	As inner-members at the state level
National Level	As inner-members at the national level	Work related to foreign affairs	As inner-members at the national level	Work related to foreign affairs

Such an arrangement, which provides for the dual role of elected representatives, as inner-members at their level and as legislative outer-members of the immediately higher level, has advantages:

1) It establishes a continuity across the levels of administration concerning legislation.

2) It provides for interaction between the legislative outer-members of a given level for sharing their common issues as inner-members of their lower level.

3) The nine inner-members and the forty-five legislative outer-members of an administrative unit together constitute the electoral college for the election of the inner-members of that level. This arrangement simultaneously provides an opportunity for assessing the legislative performances of all members, the inner-members and the legislative outer-members. That helps them in voting while electing the inner-members of that administrative unit.

4) The most important advantage, however, is that it provides an opportunity for the legislative outer-members (who are inner-members of immediately lower level) to act as an effective "opposition" or "check" to the functioning of the inner-members of that level since all legislative outer-members are also the aspirants to become inner-members of that level.

Work Schedule of Legislators

As per the proposed new model, the legislators attend legislative sessions at their level and the immediately higher level during alternate weeks. Then the question arises: How many days in a week they need to have legislative sessions? *Four-days-a-week* legislative sessions might be ideal. The rest *three* days could be used both for *fieldwork* and as a *break or holiday*. At the highest administrative level or national level, however, legislators would have *four-days-a-week* legislative sessions in one week and no legislative session in the next week as there will not be an administrative unit higher to the national level. Therefore, the national-level legislators would have *three* days in one week and all the *seven* days in another week for *work related to* foreign affairs, fieldwork, and as a break. This work schedule for the legislators would require, except for the legislators at the national level, traveling up and down to the place of legislative sessions of the immediately higher level, once in two weeks. To avoid this traveling, it would be worth exploring the feasibility of holding the sessions through video conferencing.

ASSESSMENT OF PERFORMANCE OF LEGISLATORS BY THE VOTERS — LIVE TELECAST OF LEGISLATIVE SESSIONS

As per the proposed model of democracy, legislators perform only one function—that is, legislation—unlike the existing systems wherein legislators also have executive duties. Further, as per the new model, legislators perform the legislative functions only during the legislative sessions in the Legislative House and not any other time nor anywhere else. All that the voters need to assess is the legislative performance of the legislators during legislative sessions. Hence, all the legislative sessions at all levels of administration must be telecast live for the voters, including the ordinary voters at the lowest administrative units. This arrangement helps the voters to assess the legislators continuously. Another advantage of this is that the need for election campaign by legislators and legislator aspirants is obviated to a great extent. It won't be surprising if the election campaign becomes redundant under the proposed model of democracy. Reduction or elimination of election campaigns, in turn, will reduce or eliminate election campaign expenses. That, in turn, would make it feasible to introduce yet another vital election reform—State funding of election campaign (dealt in a subsequent section).

Furthermore, as election campaign expenses are the main reason for the existence of political parties, reduction or elimination of election campaigns would discourage their existence.

Movement of Legislators—Within a Legislative Body and Between Different Levels

As per the continuous voting and relay-representation methods proposed earlier, the legislative performances of the inner-members and those of the legislative outer-members are subject to continuous evaluation by voters. These voters are either ordinary voting citizens or legislators of legislative bodies, except the highest or national. Accordingly, these voters could keep changing their votes as per the proposed "continuous voting" system. The resulting legislators' movement—the inner-members and the legislative outer-members—within a legislative body and between different levels needs some elaboration.

The movement of legislators due to change in votes is periodical (once in a month for the legislators of the lowest level and once in six months for those the higher levels), as previously suggested. Within a legislative body, a legislative outer-member, thus, can anytime move, periodically, up the ladder and replace an inner-member who, meanwhile, moves down to become the legislative outer-member. An inner-member can also move up to become an inner-member of the legislative body of the higher level. Conversely, an inner-member, of other than the lowest level, can move down and back to their lower level, where they become the inner-member again. In that case, the member at the bottom of the inner-members at that level would move down to become the inner-member of the immediately lower level.

STATE FUNDING OF ELECTION CAMPAIGNS

Since election campaign costs are enormous, if it is left to the candidates to finance their own campaign, as has been the practice, the rich would have the edge over the poor in winning the elections. As a result, political talents among the poor go mostly untapped. Moreover, elected candidates tend to become corrupt in order to recover the expenses of not only the previous elections but of the future. Besides, politicians and businesspersons or corporates tend to form an unethical nexus between them' with the former favoring the latter's business interests through legislation and the latter funding the former in elections. Self-funding of elections gives rise to yet another evil, namely, party politics. Since candidates are able to collect more funds when they are organized into a party than when they do it as independents, it follows that they tend to form or join "parties"—the political parties. In other words, the primary reason for the existence of political parties is the necessity of fund collection for fighting elections. In such a setup, it is natural that corporates would establish the nexus with political parties rather than with individual politicians. This nexus, then, would be of larger scale, more formidable, and, therefore, more dangerous than that with individual politicians. Besides, because of the party system, politicians who have contributed or collected more funds, and not necessarily those who have the more political acumen, would have more say in the affairs of the party and, if they come to power, also in the governance.

So, there should be *State funding* of election campaigns. It should be cautioned, however, that funding should not be on the lines of what, for example, Germany is following. There, the State refunds the candidates' election expenses without it being directly involved in providing the means of the campaign. Also, only the established parties are funded, which unduly discourages new parties and the independent candidates. Thus, 1) *funding should be for all candidates,* 2) *State should itself arrange for the various means and instruments of the campaign* (like newspapers, pamphlets, posters, public platforms, and TV interviews), and 3) *campaigning by means other than what is arranged by the State should be made illegal.*

Further, as noted before, the State needs to live-telecast all the proceedings of legislative sessions at all levels of administration, including the local. This measure would help the voters assess elected representatives' legislative performances more accurately, which would significantly reduce the need for other means of the election campaign by the candidates. Also, it makes campaigning not only economical, and hence more feasible, but uniform and, therefore, fair for all the candidates.

State funding, however, should be modified to suit the new methods of the election suggested in the preceding sections, namely, relay-voting and continuous voting. Besides, relay-voting, in the new system, would make the political campaigning further easy and economical for electing legislative bodies at all levels except maybe the lowest. In turn, reducing costs makes it more feasible for the introduction of State funding of election campaigns.

(Thus the leading causes of corruption in the current societies are, one, lack of separation of the legislative from the executive function, and two, candidates funding their own election campaign. The proposed democratic reforms have now addressed all these causes.)

SECRET OR OPEN BALLOT?

As noted by John Stuart Mill (a 19th century political philosopher), "voting should not be secret, because the voter is a trustee for the public whose act should be publicly known." However, this should not apply to ordinary citizens as they are vulnerable to coercion by people like the head of their family, employer, and the candidate. A legislator, on the other hand, has voting functions on several occasions—during legislation, in the election of the speaker, and, as in this new system, in the election of legislators for the higher administrative level. They, being people's representatives, should perform their voting under the eye and criticism of the public just like their performance of any other public function. In other words, a legislator should use open ballot in all their duties, which involve voting.

LEGISLATIVE BODIES AT LOWER ADMINISTRATIVE LEVELS

It is well accepted, in theory, that administrative units should have all the three governance organs at all levels. What is generally in practice, however, is that full-fledged legislative bodies exist only at higher levels of administration, say, at national and state levels but not at lower levels. This anomaly is true of both federal and unitary types of existing governments. The legislative body in a unitary government is full-fledged and all-powerful at the center but rudimentary with limited legislative powers at the state and lower levels.

In the case of a federal state, though both central and state legislative bodies are full-fledged, the lower ones are usually rudimentary and neglected. In the three lowermost levels of governance in India—districts, taluks, and panchayats—the legislative bodies are either absent or, if present, have limited policy-making powers. This anomaly leads not only to a dictatorship of the executive (bureaucrats) at the lower levels but the concentration of power in the legislators' hands at the higher levels. Further, this curbs local leadership, local talent, and local initiative and, therefore, also the development of politics from grassroots levels, and it also alienates the masses from the legislators and political processes. All these, in turn, could create a need for the existence of political parties for apprising the ordinary people of political issues of the land and thereby invite the evils of party politics. Establishing full-fledged legislative bodies at the lowermost level, along with adopting the relay-representation method described earlier, would go a long way in addressing the political issues at the grassroots levels.

Therefore, full-fledged legislative bodies should exist at all levels of administration, including the lowest one.

Some Conclusions

Thus, in this new system, unlike the existing ones, legislators are not divided into "ruling" and "opposition", and there is no threat of government falling because of loss of majority. The composition of the legislative body changes gradually and smoothly. All these conform to true democratic principles and would pave the way to evolve a State organism so adaptable, flexible, and automatically self-compensating and balancing.

THE LEGISLATURE—FUNCTION, POWERS, AND PROCEDURES

Having considered how the legislative body is to be formed, let us now see its functions and how it should be performed.

* Functions of the Legislature
* Other Powers and Functions of the Legislature
* Election of the Speaker
* Functions of the Speaker
* Emoluments and Service Conditions of Legislators

FUNCTIONS OF THE LEGISLATURE

Policies or laws are made by the legislature (interpreted by the judiciary and executed by the executive). Thus, the legislature is the policy-making body. Since elected representatives constitute it in democratic nations, it is also the political body. It is concerned throughout with the problems of the people. It determines their destiny by expressing their sovereign will as laws or policies.

The legislative body, in this new system, would necessarily have two functions: 1) legislation and 2) voting for the election of the legislative body of the immediately higher administrative unit. (Relay-representation, a new method of representation explained previously, necessitates this second function. However, for obvious reasons, this second function is not there for the highest legislative body—that is, at the national level.)

The legislative body should perform only these functions. It is also essential that all legislation should take place only within legislative sessions and nowhere else.

OTHER POWERS AND FUNCTIONS OF THE LEGISLATURE

Apart from the legislative power, the legislature also has some powers concerned with the executive and judiciary functions. It has the right or power to utilize the expertise of the executive or civil servants by way of, say, setting up expert or fact-finding commissions. Also, the legislature has the right to inspect, interrogate, or censure the civil servants or to revoke any ordinance of the executive that the legislature believes unwarranted; though, at the same time, it cannot interfere with day-to-day executive functions.

Since the legislature should be the head of the State or administrative unit, as argued in a previous section, the legislature should also have the following judicial and diplomatic powers in addition to the above executive powers.

1) judicial power—relating to the granting of pardons, reprieves, and so on, to those convicted of crimes
2) diplomatic power—diplomatic deliberation with dignitaries of other administrative units or foreign countries.

ELECTION OF THE SPEAKER

Since the discussion and voting have to be proper and systematic, there arises the need for the selection, among the members, of a speaker for conducting and moderating legislative proceedings.

The speaker is chosen by election among the inner-members. (The speaker, therefore, is also the leader of the House.) Voting for the election of the speaker should be by continuous voting. That means, as explained before, that the performance of the speaker would be subject to a continuous assessment by other members who have the right to change their votes as and when they desire. A continuous vote-register should be maintained, and the results of voting should be freshly effective for each legislative session. Since the number of legislators is quite small (nine, as proposed), to get meaningful results, each voter must vote for anybody other than themself.

Functions of the Speaker

The usual practice of assigning the speaker with the function of only moderatorship and taking away their rights to participate in discussions and voting is not proper. It unduly prevents the House from gaining the services of a member who is as good as to be elected as a speaker. Thus, in addition to moderatorship, the speaker should retain the functions of discussion (very much like the practice of moderation in scientific conferences) and voting as well.

Emoluments and Service Conditions of Legislators

The emoluments and service conditions of legislators should be generous and liberal. They should depend upon the duration and level of their service and their position in the legislative body—inner or outer. Attractive emoluments are a necessity mainly because of the decisive role of the political system in human welfare and because drawing lesser emoluments can easily be an excuse for legislators to go corrupt.

Dealing Further Blows to Party Politics

How divesting the popularly elected of its executive function, State funding of elections, multimember constituency, and restriction of voting of ordinary people to the local levels counter the evils of party politics are already discussed. We shall now see what more can be done to root out this political ill.

The State, in principle, should not recognize any political party. However, it cannot, at the same time, ban their existence. It follows, therefore, that the State should not offer any legal sanction to anti-defection measures or party-whip and should not tag the legislators as "ruling" and "opposition". In any case, in this new system of "continuous election," there is no need for any anti-defection measures. If the defection of the elected to another party is not to the liking of the voters, they can always change their votes and terminate their membership in the legislative body. Election symbols, if needed, should be given only to individual candidates and not to parties. The need for election symbols, if at all, in the new system, is only at the local level where the voters are common people and not at higher levels where the voters are legislators themselves. However, in the State-sponsored election campaign of the new system, a candidate should be allowed to mention their party affiliation, if any.

Allthesemeasureswouldshowtheexistingpoliticalpartiestheir right place, as voluntary political organizations for social service in political fields, as which they may still have a useful role to play.

POLITICAL EDUCATION AND PARTICIPATION OF THE MASSES IN THE POLITICAL PROCESSES

*The price good people pay for their indifference
to public affairs is to be ruled by evil men.*

—PLATO

*If liberty and equality, as is thought by some, are chiefly
to be found in democracy, they will be best attained when
all persons alike share in the government to the utmost.*

—ARISTOTLE

Any political reform is incomplete if it does not address the voters' political education, primarily of the common people.

The role of literacy among the populace in the success of democracies cannot be overemphasized. That apart, the simplicity of the new political system suggested in the previous sections would itself be a significant factor in making it easy for the people to comprehend the structure and functions of their political system. Comprehension of the political system would go a long way in encouraging the political participation of the masses and, hence, the system's success. For more specific and direct measures, the function of political education should be entrusted with an autonomous body like the Election Commission. One important action that the commission should take up is the introduction of political education at early schooling. Organizing political campaigns of political candidates should be another essential task of the commission. Lastly, the commission should also see that the proceedings of the legislative bodies are made public through various media: newspapers, television, and so on. This measure, in addition to bringing transparency to legislative conduct, also helps the voters continuously assess and compare legislators' performances and vote accordingly. The government should also encourage nongovernmental, voluntary political organizations to take up the cause of political education of the masses.

MAKING EXECUTIVE AND JUDICIARY AUTONOMOUS BY BRINGING INTERNAL DEMOCRACY IN THEIR ADMINISTRATIONS

In the existing democracies, both the executive and the judiciary heads are nominated by the legislators. That takes away much of the independence of the executive and the judiciary regarding their administrative decision-making and puts them at the mercy of the legislature. Therefore, there is a need to make both the executive and the judiciary fully autonomous in their administrative functions. Autonomy can be achieved by bringing internal democracy in their administration. The form of democracy they need to adopt could be on the lines of what is proposed for the legislature in the previous sections.

Administrative reforms for the executive and the judiciary, in essence, could be as follows.

The judiciary and each branch of the executive should elect a board or panel of administrators for the administrative units at the lowest level. For convenience, let us call this board, Board of Administrators (BOA). All the judges at the lowest administrative units, for example, should elect the respective BOA for the judiciary; all the engineers at the lowest administrative unit should elect the respective BOA for engineers; and so for doctors, police, accountants, and so on.

The BOAs of the lowest level should then elect BOAs for the next higher level and so on till the election of BOA for the highest level—that is, at the national level. This election system is precisely like the relay-election proposed for the elections of legislators.

The BOAs should be elected by continuous voting similar to the elections of legislators.

All discussions, deliberations, and decision-making by the BOAs should be on the lines of what is proposed for legislative sessions. Instead of "Chairperson", the moderator for sessions of BOAs may be called "Chairperson".

In addition to administrative decision-making, the BOAs at the lowest administrative units should also have the responsibility of recruiting fresh employees to their respective fields.

Transition of the Legislature, the Executive and the Judiciary to the New System from the Existing Ones

Transition of the Legislative System

The transition to the proposed new democratic system would involve, at least, two measures: 1) educating the masses about the new system and 2) relocating the existing political leaders or legislators into the new system.

An autonomous Election Commission is by far the best body to educate the masses about the new democratic system.

All existing political leaders or legislators, whatever their present level (national, state, and so on) would have to contest and win the election at the lowest level, the local legislative body, first and then get elected for higher levels as it would be a relay-election in the new system.

TRANSITION OF THE EXECUTIVE AND THE JUDICIARY SYSTEMS

The executive and the judiciary transition to the proposed new model would be similar to that of the legislature involving two measures—1) educating the workforce of the executive and the judiciary about the new system and 2) relocating them into the new system.

Each person of the existing workforce of the executive and the judiciary would have to first register themself under an administrative unit of the lowest level. The integration of the existing workforce into the new system may be decided democratically by the administrators (BOAs) of the respective administrative units.

Democracy under COBE

THE FORM OF DEMOCRACY, IN structure and function, for the proposed COBE, will be the same as that proposed for capitalism in the previous chapter. However, organizing and operation of democracy under COBE will be simpler and more straightforward. That is because there will not be scope for private wealth or money in COBE. So, there will not be scope even for corruption, party fund, crony capitalism, corporate oligarchy, or party politics.

How to Bring about the Transition to COBE

THE MORE THE NUMBER OF countries adopts the proposed COBE, the better for all people in the world. *So, the ultimate goal is to establish COBE all over the world.*

All decisions, while bringing the transition to COBE, will be made by a democratic process. First of all, therefore, a democratic system is established in society on the lines of what is proposed in the previous chapter. Creating the reformed democratic system entails, as the very first step, territorial re-delineation of the society as administrative units at different levels as proposed in that chapter. All decisions about how the transition will be brought about are then arrived at based upon public interaction mediated by elected representatives.

First of all, people will have to be prepared mentally for the transition to COBE and the challenges that come with it so that all will work in a concerted manner toward its realization. The better informed the public, the smoother the transition. People will have to be informed in an acceptable way using all media about this new direction.

First, information needs to be collected from people about their needs for various goods and services and employment interests. In this new system, one has to note that people will have the freedom to choose, both jobs of their interests and residential units of their liking. (But one has to bear in mind, as described earlier, that not only people's needs will be met free of cost, but there will be no compulsion on people to be employed. Employment will be voluntary.) A survey of the society will have to be done about the available resources—arable land, residential units, educational institutions, healthcare units, technical personnel, production plants, and so on. The use of computers and the internet will make such an endeavor easy. Further, it will be easier to proceed with the creation of the desired social design if a cybernated system is adopted to gather information about what is required and what is available. (Refer to Chapter 12 to know more about 'cybernated system'.)

During the early periods of transition from capitalism to COBE, the scarce consumer goods and services will be distributed to people in rations. The labor and material that would be saved because of changing to COBE could be invested in the productions of the scarce consumer items. Therefore, eventually, even the ration system could be done away with. The primary initial task will be to provide clean sources of energy, food, medical care, shelter, transportation system, industries for material production, education, and occupational and professional training.

The latest and advanced science, technology, and architecture will be utilized in realizing the transition to COBE. In doing so, utmost care will be given to protect the ecology. Science and technology will be used to the full potential to provide public health, create material abundance, reduce the human work maximally, and thus, improve the quality of human life to a high standard. Note that the constraints for the utilization of newer technologies will not be there in the proposed COBE model, unlike the present capitalist system.

The cities, industrial units, and the whole society under COBE must be designed by employing a *systems approach* at all levels—local, regional, and global. That is, each part or structure of a city (or an industrial unit) needs to be taken as structurally and functionally dependent upon the rest of the city and the society as a whole; each part or structure of society needs to be considered as structurally and functionally reliant on the rest of society and the world as a whole.

The new society would be designed by totally integrating all its constituent parts—production units of clean, renewable sources of energy, distribution centers, education centers, healthcare delivery system, transportation, agriculture, waste recycling, sports, entertainment, and so on. Therefore, designing and creation of all these would be by an interdisciplinary team of professionals like scientists, engineers, architects, material scientists, computer analysts, environmentalists, sociologists, educationists, healthcare scientists, behavioral scientists, and such others. Also, research sections of all universities will need to collaborate with these professionals in all these activities.

Clean energy will come from solar, wind, heat concentrators, photovoltaic, wave, biomass, geothermal, and other sources. The use of fossil fuels will be entirely done away with.

In addition to residences, cities will have goods distribution stores (both central and local), eating places, and hospitals (both central or referral and local). Each city will have a university, under which many schools will function. Cities will provide not only resources and information but have centers for art, music, sports, hobbies, and other recreations. In a COBE, cities will be created such that people will get opportunities to engage in travel, exploration, creative arts, crafts, and all kinds of research and development, to develop hidden potential, individuality, and creativity. Such a city, ultimately, allows people pursue their passions and dreams.

Currently available advanced technologies will be used to make transportation energy-efficient but eco-sustaining, and rapid but safe. The emphasis would be given to mass transit (more than small vehicles) and self-driven vehicles. Maglev train is one such example that could replace most of the aircraft.

Abundance in food production will be achieved by employing automated, high efficiency, low-energy, and low-impact cultivation methods such as vertical farming technology, aquaculture, aeroponics, aquaponics, and hydroponics.

Desalinization processes could be used to achieve an abundance of freshwater from the sea.

Education in a COBE society, as noted in an earlier chapter, will give more emphasis on basic science, history, geography, biology (including evolution, human biology, and behavior science), and communication skills in a way that will make children responsible and caring citizens. More emphasis will also be given to problem-based learning, hands-on experience, and learning from interacting directly with the physical surroundings. People will be educated not only about the proposed COBE system but about the importance of a healthy ecosystem. The transition from the current model to the COBE one, in any case, will automatically transform the education system in such ways as mentioned above because most of the educational ills of the present society are the direct consequence of the faults and restraints of capitalism.

The details of how exactly to carry out the everyday business of a COBE society will have to be considered only when the time comes for the society for the transition to COBE.

Finally, when it comes to transitioning to a COBE order, all organizations and movements whose ideas of social reconstruction are similar to the one proposed in this book, need to come together and work together. World Socialist Movement (WSM), Resource Based Economy (RBE) of The Venus Project, Natural Law Resource Based Economy (NLRBE) of The Zeitgeist Movement, and The Money Free Party (an international political party) need to work together on this regard.

WSM believes in both *collective ownership* and *democracy*. RBE and NLRBE believe in *collective ownership*. They also have done much research on technological and industrial aspects of society building. Their contribution to the transition would be of considerable help.

However, both WSM and RBE believe that the new economic order cannot be established in isolation in a single country and that it has to be done globally when all the countries accept it.

CHAPTER 20

Feasibility of a Single Nation or a Very Few Nations in the World Adopting the COBE

Is it feasible if a *single nation or a very few nations adopt the COBE?*

Yes. It is. And, it is far more likely that it is going to happen that way in all probability.

Wouldn't other nations, especially war-mongering neighbor countries, attack the COBE nation in such a case?

In such a case, the single COBE country need not dismantle its military force. In any case, the COBE country would need to go for a peaceful settlement by diplomacy rather than warring.

No one, in the proposed COBE, would want to opt to be a soldier because employment will be voluntary. Then what?

The COBE nation in question can employ high-technology soldierless defense systems—building high walls at the international border and making use of electronic surveillance, robots, drones, space satellites, and so on. In any case, at least countries not having war-mongering neighbors can readily change over to COBE.

No country is entirely self-sufficient in resources, and also, COBE nations cannot trade with nonCOBE nations as they don't have a monetary system. So, how will the COBE country sustain itself?

A COBE nation, even if it's the only nation adopting COBE in the world, can still trade (import and export) with other nations by using the currency of other nations or by having its own currency exclusively for transactions with foreign countries. Moreover, it is highly probable that foreigners will be curious about COBE and will want to visit the COBE country, which then will have a booming tourism business.

Once a single country embraces a COBE, other countries will be watching it enthusiastically. It can be safely predicted that the chances of other countries falling in line would be very high. Other countries will begin to understand the merit of the new model and will demand to adopt it and take part in it. This process of joining expands the resources, and also, there would be more benefits by economies of scale, and, over time, the world will unite.

CHAPTER 21

Action Plan to Establish Collective Ownership Based Economy—Conclusions

THE ULTIMATE GOAL IS TO establish collective ownership based economy (COBE) in place of the current capitalism or private ownership based economy (POBE) globally. That is, bring in COBE in place of POBE all over the world.

The action plan to establish a global COBE system could be as follows.

1) Convince all people about the advantages of the proposed COBE by democratic processes.
2) The campaign for the system change needs to be done by appealing to people's reason, cooperativeness, and compassion.
3) The rich, who are a minority, need to be convinced by pointing at the benefits that even they would have if the society were to transition to the COBE model.
4) The poor, who are a majority, need to be convinced mainly that economic equality is the most basic human right issue so that they demand it.

5) There will be a need to generate and mobilize support for all nonviolent movements and activism concerned with advancement and reforms in socialist and democratic practices and policies.

6) There will be a need to support the countries that go for a transition to the COBE model.

7) Last, but not least, all global forces, movements, and activism who agree with the COBE model or whose ideas are similar, including socialist and socialist-like ideas, need to join hands and act in a concerted manner during the execution of the action plan to establish the new economic model.

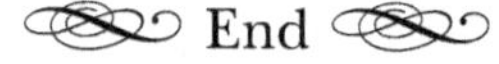 End

1. The New Human Rights Movement: Reinventing the Economy to End Oppression, Book by Peter Joseph
2. Free Online Resources
   a) The Zeitgeist Movement
   b) Frequently Asked Questions—The Venus Project
   c) FAQ—World Socialist Movement
   d) Money Free Party USA, on YouTube
   e) "Imagine"—by John Lennon, on YouTube

INDEX

ABOUT THE AUTHOR

H Prathapchandra Kedilaya, who lives in India, did his graduation in medicine with an MBBS degree and continued to practice for five years as a general practitioner. Later he did his post-graduation (MD) in Medical Biochemistry. He then taught Biochemistry in Medical Schools and managed the Clinical Biochemistry Laboratory of the hospitals attached to these Schools.

He conceptualized 'collective ownership based economy' on his own when he was in his teens, and his family supported his concept. With the advent of the internet, he discovered that more people around the world shared his thoughts, and this led him to write this book, which is his first.

9 798680 700730